awk Throwing

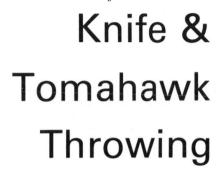

Knife &
Tomahawk
Throwing

TUTTLE Publishing

Tokyo | Rutland, Vermont | Singapore

Published by Tuttle Publishing, an imprint of Periplus Editions (HK) Ltd.

www.tuttlepublishing.com

Library of Congress Catalog Card Number: 88050409
ISBN 978-0-8048-1542-0

Distributed by:

North America, Latin America, & Europe
Tuttle Publishing
364 Innovation Drive
North Clarendon, VT 05759-9436 U.S.A.
Tel: 1 (802) 773-8930
Fax: 1 (802) 773-6993
info@tuttlepublishing.com
www.tuttlepublishing.com

Asia Pacific
Berkeley Books Pte. Ltd.
3 Kallang Sector #04-01
Singapore 349278
Tel: (65) 6741-2178
Fax: (65) 67414-2179
inquiries@periplus.com.sg
www.periplus.com

Japan
Tuttle Publishing
Yaekari Building, 3rd Floor
5-4-12 Osaki, Shinagawa-ku
Tokyo 141 0032
Tel: (81) 3 5437-0171
Fax: (81) 3 5437-0755
sales@tuttle.co.jp
www.tuttle.co.jp

23 22 21 20 19   16 15 14 13 12   1904MP
Printed in Singapore

TUTTLE PUBLISHING® is a registered trademark of Tuttle Publishing, a division of Periplus Editions (HK) Ltd.

Dedicated to the memory of my friend
FRANK DEAN

In addition to his many outstanding accomplishments
as a great cowboy champion-performer
with horses, whips, and ropes,
he was the first famous professional
to reveal to backyard knife-throwers
the many secrets of professional knife throwing.

Table of Contents

List of Figures

9

Preface

IT HAS BEEN a lifelong preoccupation with knives and other edged weapons that has determined, first as a hobby, the main thrust of this writer's life. From the age of 14 when I first threw my opened Barlow knife at a passing skunk while on a camping trip (and amazingly enough scored a bull's-eye), I've enjoyed the sport. It must be reported that the skunk also scored a bull's-eye with a perfect squirt against the young hunter before it expired, and to this day I cannot stand the aroma of skunk.

As a youth, the art of knife throwing was a growing interest that in later years would expand to include the designing and crafting of professional quality throwing-knives. In time, this sideline helped to provide for a growing family, and eventually became a viable business that is known in the cutlery world as the Tru-Balance Knife Company.

It seemed that at the time this avocation of making throwing-knives got started, very few people knew much at all about the subject, aside from a handful of professionals and a few sportsman students of the art. So, mostly by trial and error, I taught myself the basics of the sport, the proper throwing-knife designs, and the ballistics thereof, and then I was on my way.

In the summer of 1944, as a sergeant in an Army Air Corps detachment stationed for a while at the old U.S. Rubber Company plant in Detroit, the author sought out and became friends with both the company metallurgist and the blacksmith. These two gentlemen showed me the basics of knife making, including the forging, grinding, and heat treating of steel blades. Using the company's fine facilities, I produced my first throwing-knife that summer, a project that was jokingly called a "government job!"

After the war, much of my spare time was devoted to both designing, developing, and crafting throwing-knives, and to becoming more proficient in the art of throwing. Being a trained journalist also, I began to write articles and books about knives and knife throwing—many of which were published during the sixties and seventies.

To write a book like this, however, does require considerable help from friends, a number of whom are noted professional knife throwers of the present day. Their help has been invaluable.

My special tribute goes to the late Frank Dean, who, in 1937, wrote and published a 24-page booklet called *The Art of Knife Throwing*. Although distribution was very limited, it was, nevertheless, the first book to reveal the secrets of the professionals to sportsmen knife-throwers lucky enough to obtain a copy. In 1980, Frank Dean's latest book, *Cowboy Fun,* was published, and one chapter in this fascinating book deals entirely with knife throwing and the professionals of past and present who became the greats in the "art of impalement." Frank Dean, in addition to being one of the world's greatest knife throwers, was a world champion cowboy rope-twirler and established several records documented in the *Guinness Book of World Records*.

George E. (Skeeter) Vaughan, acknowledged as the foremost tomahawk thrower of the present day as well as being a great professional knife thrower, has contributed much to my knowledge of the twin sports, as has Paul LaCross, an amazing showman who personally taught me the true art of the professionals some 20 years before these lines were written.

Other "pros" in the business have also been most helpful and cooperative, including Sylvester Braun, Kenneth (Che Che) Pierce, Larry Cisewski, and several lesser-known artists with the throwing-knife whom I have had the pleasure of working with in a coaching capacity and in making for them the knives they perform with in their acts.

Many of the photos shown in this book were taken by my son, Dr. Alan W. McEvoy, and by other good friends who are enthusiastic knife throwers themselves. Of considerable assistance have been Michael Woggon, Gene Austin, and Mr. W. D. (Bo) Randall and his son Gary, of Randall Made Knives. Artist Robert Irwin has also made contributions to this book, as has Mr. Eizo Shirakami, the noted martial arts authority of Japan.

My very special thanks go to Charles Houston Price, the publisher of *Knife World* and *Knife World Books,* to J. Bruce Voyles, publisher of the beautiful *Blade Magazine,* and to Oran Scurlock, Jr., publisher of *Muzzleloading Magazine.* These gentlemen have given their permission to use material in the form of passages and reprints which I wrote for these publications over the years.

HARRY K. MCEVOY

Grand Rapids, Michigan

Knife & Tomahawk Throwing

I

The Fine Points
of Knife Throwing

ALMOST EVERY adult at one time or another has watched a professional knife thrower perform in a circus or other theatrical show. It is awe-inspiring to watch the skill that is demonstrated by the pro as he hurls his big, flashing blades all around his lovely lady assistant in very close proximity to her pin-up pretty figure.

That skill didn't just happen. Granted, there must be considerable natural talent, but it is also the result of years of almost daily practice. The basic skills can be learned—and fairly quickly—by almost any determined sportsman who truly wants to become proficient in the ancient art of knife throwing. All he needs to start out with is to have the ability to throw a ball, crack a whip, fish with a casting rod, or toss a dart. With these basic skills, plus a good knife that is properly designed and balanced for throwing by either handle or blade, a suitable target, and the simple study of the fundamentals to be described herein, he is on his way to becoming a knife thrower. Once again, to become an *expert* knife thrower, however, requires that most basic element that is called: LOTS OF PRACTICE!

The first consideration is a proper throwing-knife. You must select a knife that has three important and basic features. First, it must be correctly balanced for throwing. Then, it must be long enough to provide maximum control by the thrower. Finally, it must have enough weight for good, firm target penetration.

The length of any throwing-knife, when taken into consideration with the other two elements of good design—proper weight and balance—is very important. If the knife is too light or too short, the thrower will not have perfect control. A knife designed and intended for blade throwing only can be a bit short by comparison—anywhere from 10 to 12 inches is recommended. But a true professional knife, or the handle-throwing type, should be anywhere from 11 to 16 inches in overall length. The best *average* length for these two types is 13 to 14 inches overall, depending on the width and weight of the weapon.

In 1945, this writer developed and published a formula for selecting throwing-knives which has been universally adopted and is still in use today: "A good throwing-knife, of whatever type, should average from 1 to $1\frac{1}{4}$ ounces for every inch of over-all length." For proper penetration of the target boards, the knife should weigh at least 10 ounces and not more than 16. (One notable exception to this simple weight formula is in the case of contests involving the twin sports of knife and tomahawk throwing. *See* page 32.)

Excellent and well-balanced throwing-knives are available from numerous sources in America and abroad, but the thrower should always remember the three basic features of a good throwing-knife:

1. It must be properly balanced for throwing.
2. It should be long enough for maximum control.
3. It should be heavy enough to insure good target penetration. (One ounce for every inch of overall length is a good "rule of thumb.")

A knife thrower has a choice of three different types of knives. One design is made to throw by the handle grip. It features a heavy blade, such as a Bowie type, but with a light handle, and a balancing point located at about overall center or up to one inch back of center.

Another type is the blade thrower. It is usually shaped like a narrow-bladed hunting knife, or short bayonet, with a heavy handle. Its balancing point is somewhere around the hilt—the area where blade and handle join. With both of the types described

1. A collection of handle throwing-knives. Several can also be thrown by the blade due to the absence of sharp edges.

2. A collection of blade throwing-knives. Some are made from old bayonets.

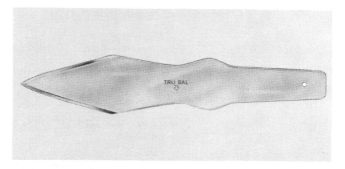

3. The "Sport Pro" professional throwing-knife.

above, you just have to remember to grasp the light end when getting ready to throw. With either type, you always throw by holding the lighter end of the knife.

The third type of knife is the true professional throwing-knife. It is this type that is preferred by most experienced backyard throwers, as well as by the professionals. It is usually perfectly center-balanced with no sharp edges to cut the hand, and it can be thrown equally well by handle or blade.

Whichever throwing-knife you choose, it should have the correct balance for the type of throwing you want to start with. (Hopefully, you will eventually be able to master all three types of throwing knives described.) It must also be heavy enough to provide good target penetration when thrown, and long enough to give you proper control as it leaves your hand.

4. The proper grip for throwing a knife by the handle.

The Handle Throw

Since the handle throw is the easiest to master because only even spins of the blade are involved, consider this throwing technique first. Here, the handle is grasped firmly in the same natural manner in which you would normally pick up a hammer or hatchet, keeping the plane of the blade vertical. The thumb should be extended along the top edge of the knife, so that it becomes a "pointer" which will tend to greatly increase your accuracy as you practice. The weapon is then hurled overhand in a simple "hatchet throw" that allows for one full turn of the knife.

The thrower should remember to keep the plane of the blade vertical as it slips from his hand, and to avoid any wrist snap. In other words, it should be released as if it is *hot,* in order to prevent that snapping of the wrist which could ruin the throw. If the knife is properly made for throwing, it will take a natural turn in about 10 to 12 feet from where it slips from the hand. The thrower should stand about 15 feet back from the target, since up to three or four feet may be taken up with the mechanics of the throw. The throw itself should be hard and fast and straight, making sure the plane of the knife is vertical as it leaves your hand.

The results of that first throw by the handle are not too important, because before real proficiency is developed, the thrower must first understand and master the mechanics of the throw. These basic elements include the *stance, wind-up, throw,* and *follow-through.*

The Stance. Assuming the thrower is right-handed, the stance can be one of two distinct placements of the feet. If you want to throw with full power and velocity, put your right foot forward on the "mound" like a baseball pitcher so that when you throw, you step out with your left foot and swing your entire body forward in the throwing movement. This is called the "sportsman's stance." It is especially good for speed and maximum target penetration, and is the stance assumed by hunters who throw knives

5. The professional stance for throwing by the handle grip.

over long, multiple-spin distances at game animals in that fascinating hunting sport.

The other stance, called the "professional stance," is the one used by most backyard throwers, as well as being the one assumed by professionals who throw knives for a living. A major advantage of this stance is that it brings the thrower one long pace or more closer to the target. If you are right-handed, place

6. The professional stance for throwing by the blade grip.

your left foot forward, right foot back, and sink into a sort of half crouch. Your weight should be balanced on the balls of your feet. Regardless of which stance you use—sportsman or professional—the distance to the target from where you take your stance should always be measured from the placement of your back foot. Left-handed throwers can adapt these instructions to their own style of throwing.

The Wind-up and Throw. The wind-up consists of simply bringing the knife back by your head and whipping it forward in a throwing motion. As mentioned earlier, release the knife as if it were hot so that you make sure not to snap your wrist. Let your instincts guide you as to when you should release the knife—when you reach that exact split-second the knife is lined up with the target.

The Follow-through. This is the continuation of the throwing movement after the knife has been released and is spinning toward the bull's-eye. As knife-throwing experts all agree, the follow-through is the secret to guiding the weapon accurately to the target.

If the thrower is using a knife properly designed and balanced for throwing and is standing at the correct distance for the handle throw herein described, the knife should turn once in the air and then strike the target, point first, and straight in.

If the knife hits the target flat, with the point up, just step backward a foot or two so that it can complete its turn to stick point first. If it hits flat with the point down, you are too far back and must step forward a foot or so. If it hits handle-end first, you must experiment stepping backward or forward until you find that exact distance needed for a perfect stick. Once you find that ideal spot, be sure to mark it in some way—driving a stake or digging a toe hole perhaps. Then stand on that same spot for a perfect throw each time at that particular distance. This is a simple trial and error method which all throwers must follow in order to determine the exact distance from the target they must stand for successful throws. It varies, of course, with each different thrower. For example, because of their long arms, tall people usually need a bit more throwing room than shorter throwers.

The Blade Throwing-Knife

The throwing-knife that is designed and balanced to be thrown by the blade usually features a slender, lightweight blade with a heavy handle. Its balancing point is somewhere within one inch either way from the hilt, and it usually has only one true cutting edge, although it may feature a "false edge" on top that is cosmetic and would not normally cut the hand. Commercial-type hunting knives should not be thrown, since they are usually too brittle to stand the shock. A throwing-knife of any type should be correctly designed and tempered so that it will *never* break—even after a lifetime of regular use.

To throw a sharp-bladed knife (with only one cutting edge) by the blade, you grasp the blade firmly with the cutting edge *away* from the palm of your hand. Your thumb should point directly toward the handle. Line up your first, second, and third fingers on the opposite side of the blade, while the little finger, which is too small to be of much use on

7. Blade grip on sharp-edged knife showing thumb placement.

a narrow blade, can be curled up to one side and thus kept out of the way. From the bottom tip of the point, about one inch of steel should protrude. This will bring the point to within a half-inch of the crease in the skin where hand and wrist are joined. It will also permit much better control of the knife than would be possible if it were grasped at the very tip of the point in a poor and ineffective "pinch grip."

The throw is made using the same throwing movement as described for the handle throw. However, the blade throwing-knife can be up to two or three inches shorter than either the handle throwing-type or the true professional models. With its narrow blade, the blade throwing-knife is best thrown with the plane of the blade horizontal—leaving the hand with the blade parallel to the ground and not vertical, as is done with the other two types of throwing-knives.

8. Blade grip on sharp-edged knife showing thumb and finger alignment.

9. Blade grip on sharp-edged knife showing finger alignment.

With a blade-thrower, your distance to the target will be for a ½ spin, a 1½ spin, etc. You will need to stand back an additional four feet or so for that extra half turn in the 1½-spin throw. (The ½ spin is not recommended for the average sportsman thrower, although many professionals often use it for close quarter "speed throwing" by the blade.)

Accuracy can be developed more quickly if the thrower concentrates on just the $1\frac{1}{2}$-spin throw.

The Professional Throwing-Knife

The third style of knife is the true professional throwing model, which is usually perfectly center-balanced and has no sharp edges to cut the hand. It is simple in design—usually a diamond-shaped or leaf-shaped point which tapers all the way back to the end of the handle. There is no extending cross-piece or guard to mar the symmetrical lines of the knife from front to back. This absence of a crosspiece on a knife used by a professional is due to the fact that such a crosspiece could possibly cause a bad bounce by another knife and injure his assistant, around whom he hurls those bright, flashing blades.

A true professional throwing-knife is thrown equally well by handle or blade using the professional style of throwing. It is *always* thrown with the plane of the blade vertical and hurled without any deviations on every throw. Only the distance to the target changes, depending upon which grip—handle or blade—is used. Grasp either the handle or the blade in the same way for either full even turns, or the $\frac{1}{2}$, $1\frac{1}{2}$, and $2\frac{1}{2}$ turns, or from as far back as one can successfully stick the knife.

To throw a double spin by the handle, or $2\frac{1}{2}$ spins by the blade grip, simply move back an additional three paces from your previous distances. You can estimate that it takes you those three extra

10. Correct grip for blade throw in the professional style, with no sharp edges to cut the hand.

11. Center-balanced professional throwing-knife without a crosspiece.

paces for each additional spin—even if you are throwing quadruple turns.

No matter how you hurl the knife, and regardless of the distance thrown, in order for the blade to stick correctly, it must *always* penetrate the target wood with the plane of the blade *vertical* and *not* crossways to the grain of the target boards.

Big Bowie-style Knives/Tomahawks

As previously mentioned, one exception to the "1 to 1¼ ounces for every inch of overall length" formula for selecting knives concerns the black-powder shooting enthusiasts—the muzzleloaders—who stage most of the contests involving the twin sports of knife and tomahawk throwing. Since many of the tomahawks hurled in these contests will weigh up to 1¾ pounds, some black-powder knife-throwers seem to want a big Bowie-style knife for handle throwing which matches their tomahawk in overall weight. They then throw both weapons in the same way and from the same distance for one or more even spins.

Those big Bowie-style knives throw more like a tomahawk or hatchet, and with a fairly slow spin. Like a tomahawk, such a knife can be hurled with considerable accuracy, if not with great speed. In fact, I have often recommended to beginning knife throwers that they first take an hour off to master tomahawk or hatchet throwing, because usually it is much easier to learn than is knife throwing. By doing so, the thrower can more quickly grasp the fundamentals and the throwing ballistics involved in both weapons.

The professional style of throwing, which has been explained herein, is also the one most expert tomahawk throwers adopt. Thus, when you start practicing with both knives and 'hawks, it is recommended that you assume the professional stance

12. Tomahawk and throwing-knife—a matching set used for competitive throwing.

as previously described, or start with both feet together, then simply step forward with the left foot for the wind-up, release, and follow-through.

Making Your Own Knife

If you, as a knife-throwing enthusiast, have access to facilities for sawing or grinding out a knife, it is fairly easy to make your own—or even a matched set. First make a drawing on cardboard of the design you prefer. This should be the exact size of the model you plan to produce. As you cut it out with a pair of scissors, work on the design so as to make it balance properly for the type of throwing you plan to do. The cardboard design will balance out the same way when made up in flat steel bar stock.

At your local steel warehouse—or even sometimes a junkyard—get a bar of steel 1 to 2 inches wide and about 12 to 16 inches long. Saw or grind to a good point, sharpen the edges, and taper the handle back for a smooth release. Make sure there is no flare at the back end which could cause the knife to hang in your hand when released and thus spoil your throw. A knob or any ornamental protrusion at the end of the handle is fine only for a knife intended for the blade grip which could use the extra weight where it will do the most good. For a throwing-knife designed for the handle grip, however, it is best to have the handle smooth and tapered back so that it will slip from your hand smoothly with no hang-up at the release.

For a handmade throwing-knife of your own design and craftsmanship, it is nice to have the steel properly tempered for throwing, although this is not really essential. A blade made from common cold-rolled steel may bend a bit on a bad throw, but with a few judicious hammer blows, it can easily be straightened back to shape. As for the handle, it can be made with ordinary electrician's tape, with enough windings to make the grip feel comfortable when the knife is thrown.

As pointed out, the way to become an expert knife thrower is to practice long and hard until you become as perfect as possible. There is one little tip, however, that could provide a shortcut to achieving the accuracy you are hoping for. Here is how it is done:

First, walk up to the target and place a small black circle or square of tape exactly in the center of the target face. Next, throw a knife at least a dozen times at that tiny black mark, imagining it to be a sort of super magnet that will draw your blade directly to itself on every throw.

Keep throwing and watch carefully where each knife sticks. Soon you will notice that a pattern emerges. For instance, most of your "sticks" might be concentrated at the three o'clock position, and four inches to the right of dead center.

It is now easy to correct the situation. Simply move your aiming dot or mark over to the nine o'clock position, and four inches to the left of dead center, and throw *only* at that dot and *not* at the center of the target face. This should help you achieve "bull's-eye precision," and from that time on, the black aiming dot can be strictly imaginary. With that constant practice and the "point-of-aim" technique just described, you should be able to develop your throwing skills to such a peak that you will be able to hit just about anything you throw at squarely and accurately. This system really works and that is how the professionals of knife throwing got to be just that—*professionals!*

II

How to Build Targets

IT GOES without saying that if you are going to throw a knife or tomahawk, you must have a suitable target backstop. Softwood is the best material for target boards, and if at all possible, try to avoid any wood harder than basswood. Your best source for target boards is a dealer of used lumber—there are wrecking companies who take down or demolish old houses and commercial buildings in almost every sizable community. Such firms salvage usable old beams, and wide, thick boards, and these materials make ideal target wood.

In rural communities, you could try approaching a local sawmill which specializes in roughly sawn lumber. This will often be the best source for a board target, since the wood can be custom-sawn to exactly the right thickness, width, and length.

Ideally, your target boards should be at least three

inches thick and as wide as possible; certainly it should be a minimum of 20 inches to 2 feet in width. A three-foot width is even better, since more target faces can be spread over a greater area, thus decreasing the chance for possible handle damage when several knives are thrown before any are retrieved.

Three wide boards are recommended, since the center board will take most of the punishment from the countless cuts of sharply pointed knives. This center board can easily be replaced, reversed, or exchanged with the two side boards as necessary. Remember, since a thin board will be very short-lived, it is quite important that you obtain boards that are as thick as possible.

The target should be constructed with the grain of the wood vertical. It is a good idea to nail several sturdy crosspieces across the back to hold it tightly together. Make the target at least 20 to 30 inches wide and from 3 to 6 feet in length. It should then be set up so that the tops of the boards are 5 to 6 feet from the ground, and the target should be hung, nailed, or leaned against a convenient support. Some throwers make a frame to hold the boards or else construct a special hanging target, which is what I would highly recommend.

The Hanging Target

A hanging target is easy to build. Get a couple of standard two-inch pipes (often obtainable in a local junkyard) that are eight feet long, and threaded

13. A hanging board target suspended in front of a pipe frame.

on one end. Then take a third length of pipe that is about 18 or 20 inches long and threaded on both ends, and join it to the long pipes by "elbows" so as to resemble an inverted letter U. Next take a heavy "eye bolt" and anchor it through a hole drilled in the center of the short cross-piece pipe. This will hold the target.

The bottom 18 inches or so of the long pipes are then embedded in cement to hold the frame in a permanent position. Strong, heavy staples should be used to attach a short length of stout steel chain

14. Larry Cisewski throwing at a hanging target.

across the back of the target boards, and a heavy S-hook is needed to connect the target chain to the eyebolt anchored through the crosspiece. The target itself should be wider than the distance between the vertical pipes and should hang up against the front of the frame.

The S-hook and the steel chain must be strong enough not only to hold the considerable weight of the target boards, but also to be able to withstand the heavy strain exerted when deeply embedded knives are withdrawn from the wood.

15. The recommended type of log target and stand for back-yard knife and tomahawk throwing.

The Log Target

The best of all targets, especially for the back-yard knife thrower, is not a board target at all, but a cross section from the butt end of a large log or tree trunk cut about eight or ten inches thick. The log should be as wide as possible, ideally up to about three feet in diameter.

Willow is probably the best wood for a log target, but any softwood will do. Your best source of obtaining a section would be through your local power company or tree removal service. Try to have their tree-trimming crew cut off a slab or two from the butt end the next time they bring down a willow or other softwood tree. This can be mounted on a

16. A "dream" target for knives and tomahawks, built by Danny O'Donnell of Pennsylvania.

platform or suspended from the inverted **U**-frame just described. You will then have the best of all possible target backstops for both knife and tomahawk throwing. A log target can be simply turned around to the unused side when it gets too chopped up to hold the weapon firmly, or it can easily be resurfaced with a good cross cut or chain saw. (Nothing will demolish even a log target as fast as a tomahawk or hatchet.) When the face of the log gets badly splintered around the center, it is time to resurface or turn it around.

For best results, you should place the target face, or faces, below eye-level. Furthermore, it is also a lot more fun to throw a matched set of three or six knives than it is to throw only one and then have to walk up to the target and retrieve it for the next throw. Thus, separate target faces are recommended if you plan to throw more than one knife. Otherwise you could easily nick and damage handles or blades if they are struck by successive knives. Old playing cards, paper plates, or plastic lids off empty coffee cans all make suitable target faces.

The Moving Target

In addition to the simple standard backstops of a board target or the cross section of a big log, there are various novelty targets you can construct which will add enjoyment to the sport. Perhaps the most sporting of all is the moving target, and there are several types you can construct that will offer added interest to your throwing sessions.

One involves using an old automobile tire, in which you insert thick boards that have been cut to fit inside the casing and then nailed together to remain secure within the tire itself. It can then be rolled in front of the thrower by an associate, or hung up and swung back and forth on a rope or chain, or even revolved, as the thrower attempts to score a bull's-eye on a painted circle or some other target face devised for his mark.

Another good moving target can be made of short, thick boards mounted vertically on a rectangular wooden frame, measuring perhaps about 20 inches high and 3 feet in length. Screw eyes are attached to the top of the frame so that the target can be threaded on a stout wire or rope that is positioned four or five feet above the ground. It can then be slid along the wire fairly rapidly with a shove by an associate. A bull's-eye can be painted or tacked on at the center of the target boards, thus providing a mark to throw at while the rig is in motion. Hunters often use similar targets to sharpen their aiming skills prior to the hunting season.

Throwing Games

There are a variety of simple knife and tomahawk throwing games that can provide novelty to throwing sessions where two or more throwers are participating.

One is the ancient game known in America as "Tic, Tac, Toe," and in England and other countries as "Naughts and Crosses." Here, the target boards are crossed in the usual way with string (nylon is best) tied to nails on the four sides. To avoid cutting the string with a bad or inaccurate throw, it is best to position them at least one inch in front of the board. Only knives should be used to play this fine old game if the squares are marked with string. If playing with tomahawks, which have broad cutting edges, instead of using string, use adhesive tape to mark off the squares. Combining both mental and physical skill, this game gives the participant a chance to demonstrate his ability as a marksman, while trying to outwit his opponents.

Playing cards can also be tacked up on the back-stop and throwers can compete to see who can stick the highest or best cards to make up a winning poker hand. These and other simple but interesting games which anyone can dream up will provide a great deal of fun, recreation, and competition.

✳   ✳   ✳

When the throwing session ends, it is important to remember to take care of your knives. Any nicks or cuts in the blades or handle slabs should be carefully smoothed out with a good file. The knives should be wiped with a dry cloth or paper towels (which are excellent for this purpose). The same also applies to tomahawks. Your throwing instruments—regardless of type—should always be stored in a cool, dry place that you are sure is well out of the reach of small children.

By all means, safety must always be uppermost in your mind at all times, and especially during every throwing session. Set up your target in a good open place where there is absolutely no chance of anyone approaching it from any direction unobserved. You may sometimes also need extra space to rope off the throwing area, since even in backyard practice you are liable to find every kid in the neighborhood (and even their parents) coming to watch you perform with those knives or 'hawks.

Spectators and participants alike should be kept well back of the throwing line because an improperly thrown knife or tomahawk can sometimes take a bad bounce and possibly injure someone. A knife, especially, can sometimes bounce back with considerable force directly at the thrower, at which time some very fast ducking may be required. Needless to say, a bouncing knife that nicks your anatomy can really spoil your day.

Practice sensible and careful safety precautions at all times; with this in mind, you will find these twin sports of knife and tomahawk throwing will provide some of the best recreation you have ever enjoyed.

III

Evolution of
the Throwing-Knife

ON A COOL November day in 1830, Jim Bowie
stood in a small blacksmith's shop located in the
backwoods settlement of Washington, Arkansas,
gazing with pleasure at the newly forged knife
he held in his big hand.

Here was a knife, just completed to his special
order by the smithy, that filled him with a deep
pride of ownership. This knife was destined to become the most legendary blade in all of American
history.

The design was a composite of special features
worked out not only by Jim Bowie, but by his brother
Rezin Bowie, and the blacksmith, James Black. It
was a big knife, with a heavy blade and a clipped
top edge that was sharpened like the bottom edge,
but had the shape of a sweeping concave curve. It
featured a heavy brass cross-guard to protect a man's

hand from the cutting stroke of an opponent, and was designed to cut deeply on either the forward or back stroke should a man's life depend upon it.

Jim Bowie may or may not have realized as he looked down admiringly upon his wonderful weapon that not only did he hold the finest fighting knife ever designed, he also possessed one of the best throwing-knives ever made.

It was soon to be called the "Bowie knife," and in the years that followed it became famous beyond belief, with thousands of more or less authentic "copies" pouring out from the cutlery makers of Sheffield, England and the eastern American cities to the wild American frontiers. Backwoods blacksmiths also turned their talents to forging out these suddenly popular "Bowie" knives, and from the halls of Congress to the most remote regions of the American frontier, many a gentleman, settler, trapper, soldier, riffraff, and outlaw felt slightly "undressed" without a Bowie knife within their own easy reach.

The dramatic death of Colonel Jim Bowie during the seige of the Alamo by Santa Anna in March 1836, and the supposed burning of his body and bloodied knife on the funeral pyre, further helped to spread the fame of this fabulous weapon.

From the 1830s to the present time, the classic Bowie design has been both the most popular of all blade configurations and about the best all-purpose knife that can also be thrown for sport or

17. A classic Bowie knife, with a "coffin handle" design that has been popular since the 1850s. Knife designed by Harvey McBurnette.

combat. It is by far the favorite blade of most American sportsmen, and is the type thrown most often at muzzleloading knife-throwing matches in the United States.

Although the modern sport of knife throwing has gained wide prominence only since the early 1950s, the present-day popularity of the sport is just a rebirth of the knife-throwing interest that started in the early days of the American Civil War. (Naturally, the throwing-knife most widely used at that time was of the Bowie pattern.)

Proof of this is shown in a black-and-white wood-cut drawing entitled: "Camp Life in the Confederate Army—Mississippians Practicing with the Bowie Knife." This illustration, showing a group of rebels throwing their Bowie knives at a mark on a large tree, first appeared in the August 31, 1861 issue of the old *Harper's Weekly*, when the Civil War had barely begun and Confederate hopes were high. The drawing is important since it proves that knife throwing was immensely popular among the Bowie-totin' rebels as a form of relaxation to break the monotony of camp life.

The Union Army of the North also had its devotees to the sport, and during the early years of that tragic war between the states, countless numbers of soldiers fighting on both sides carried a Bowie knife into battle.

Among the frontiersmen, especially trappers and Indian fighters, many carried a special knife just for throwing. This knife was long and narrow in the blade, but did not have a cross-guard or hilt common to the Bowie pattern. This was carried in addition to a regular "working" knife—usually a Bowie. The throwing-knife often doubled as a rifleman's knife and was usually made from an old file, which often was the best source of good steel available at that period. Backwoods blacksmiths utilized every bit of wrought iron or steel they could obtain, and since good steel was scarce, very little of the material was ever wasted.

Knives suitable for throwing have been made by crafters since the dawn of the Bronze Age. By 2500 B.C., fine bronze daggers were being crafted by the Sumerians at Ur in what was then Mesopotamia, and which is today Iraq. These knives had ribbed blades and sturdy tangs—they were exceptionally good knives for the period. The Persians also turned out beautiful daggers at their famed bronze-making centers of Luristan and Talyche. Even before 3000 B.C., the technique of making and working bronze into daggers had reached Europe, and by 2000 B.C. had spread as far north as Great Britain.

Designs would vary from region to region and maker to maker, but the long slender blades with the heavy handles were most suitable for throwing by the blade—which, up until the origin of the Bowie knife some thousands of years later—was the method most widely employed by those who threw knives for pleasure, for profession, or as was sometimes the case, for assassination.

Through the centuries that followed the Bronze Age, and as iron (and later steel) became available to blade crafters, the knife shapes for personal protection developed into three main variations. These were the dirk, the dagger, and the stiletto, with all three being nicely balanced for close-quarter self-defense. Because they all had light blades and heavy handles, when they had to be thrown, they were undoubtedly gripped by the blade and hurled handle-first.

One can speculate about the throwing qualities of the ribbed bronze daggers that were in wide use many centuries prior to the Christian era, as well as the other styles of daggers which came much later and were crafted of steel. They had various names such as rondels, baselards, quillons, and dirks, and were in use from medieval times. No doubt there were instances in distant days when a blade was thrown for sport, self-defense, or for less noble reasons, but until modern times, no records were left to document such incidents.

Most of the above-mentioned knives were all-purpose knives, and since they were expensive to purchase, almost every man had to make do with just the one he owned. An interesting example of such a knife was the ancient scramasax—a small version of a sword-like weapon, highly prized by the Vikings, the Franks, and the Saxons. Some were as much as two feet long, while others were only five or six inches in blade length. These were mostly wide, straight-bladed knives with a nicely contoured handle and no crosspiece or guard. They fitted the hand perfectly, and tapered down to a sharp point. They would have been easy to throw and were well-balanced for that purpose.

The Vikings, especially, were so fond of their scramasaxes that they kept them at hand even while they slept. When they died, these knives were usually buried with them, and samples have been found in the ancient burial mounds of those warriors who went to Valhalla. Since the Vikings were noted for throwing their war axes in combat, it must be assumed that they also threw their scramasax knives under extremely combative situations.

The long, slender fighting knives of the French, Spanish, and Italian knife wielders of the 16th, 17th, and 18th centuries were called various names, such as daggers, stilettos, and poinards. The sturdier daggers of the Scots and English were known as dirks.

The dirk normally featured a broader, sometimes double-edged blade and was usually shorter than the slender French or Italian blades. The Scottish dirk was developed in the 17th century, and like the famous scramasax of the Vikings that in many ways it resembled, it had no guard or crosspiece. It was, therefore, an excellent weapon for throwing, especially if only one of the edges was sharp.

It is difficult to generalize how these knives might have been thrown. It depended on the weight, length, and especially the balance of each individual weapon. If heavy in the handle, it would no doubt have been thrown by the blade; if the handle was light and the blade heavy, it would have best been thrown by the handle. The dirk was a common type of edged weapon in use by British officers and seamen of the 18th century, and many a knife carried as a sidearm by American frontiersmen of the period was in reality a dirk.

Another combat blade in existence from the first half of the 17th century could also be thrown, if needed, by the handle. This was called the plug bayonet.

The word bayonet, describing a knife or sword-like blade attached to the muzzle of a rifle or musket, was named after the city of Bayonne in southern France. As early as the mid-16th century, this city was famous all over Europe for the fine quality of its daggers which were called *dagues de Bayonne*— or *bayonnettes*. French troops in the vicinity of Bayonne were noted for their special plug daggers which were inserted into the muzzles of their muskets after their volley was fired and they had to repel a charge with unloaded guns.

The plug bayonet—a dagger with a tapered handle—was widely used throughout the wars of the 17th and 18th centuries, including the American Revolution. It was constructed so that it could be used as an excellent throwing knife if worst came to worst, and was a weapon that was liked especially by the British. It was well balanced to be thrown by the handle, and was not too bad when it was thrown by the blade either.

There are no available records of instances where knives were thrown in combat prior to the American Civil War. The best assumption is that such instances occurred mostly during ship-to-ship engagements in the days of sail, when vessels locked together and boarding parties swung from their ratlines to the decks of enemy ships, fought hand-to-hand, and hurled pointed marlin spikes or daggers and dirks at enemy seamen.

With regard to recent wars, it has been verified that short bayonets as well as modern throwing-knives have been hurled successfully in combat. An acquaintance of mine, a veteran of World War II who fought with the U.S. Marines in the Pacific, related how he threw his M-1 bayonet (normally used on a Garand rifle) into the back of an enemy soldier at a distance of about 20 feet, thus saving the life of a buddy. This bayonet was brought home, and is now in my own edged weapon collection. It is $14\frac{1}{2}$ inches overall, and as a blade throwing-weapon it performs well.

Latins, for the most part, seem to have an affinity for the knife, which, whether true or not, has gained them the reputation of having special skills in both knife fighting and throwing. Many Mexican knife crafters, in addition to turning out a vast amount of "junk" for the tourist trade, do sometimes make some pretty good knives—especially those with Mexican stylized Bowie patterns. Also, some professional style throwing-knives are forged by blacksmiths in Oaxaca, a city in southeastern Mexico located about 220 miles from Mexico City.

Knives with a simple but distinctive pattern were produced in Cuba during the mid-1800s by local blacksmiths who had developed a crude, but serviceable throwing-knife for combat use. This *cuchillo*

18. Throwing-knives of frontier days. *Left to right:* Cuban throwing-knife; Indian Bowie-style without crosspiece; Classic Bowie.

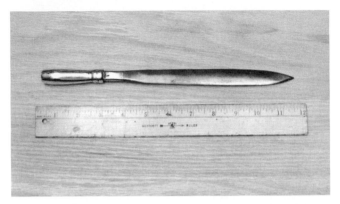

19. A Cuban knife hand-forged in Cuba during the 1860s.

was all metal, and some primitive Mexican throwing-knives look very similiar to these Cuban patterns, with their light blades and heavy handles designed for throwing by the blade grip.

The bulk of these knives were handmade during the unsuccessful revolution against Spain by the Cubans, a war which lasted from 1868 to 1878, and went down in history as the "Ten Years War." These Cuban knives were forged out of whatever steel was available. They were seldom more than 1 inch wide, with an overall length of about 12 inches. Handles were mere cylinders of brass, cast over the tang, and then rounded and smoothed with a file. They were beautifully balanced for blade throwing, and an expert thrower could nail an enemy up to 30 feet away.

20. Throwing knives spanning many decades. The six knives on the right were all designed after 1950.

The Bowie types, modified Rifleman knives, and the straight-bladed throwers similar to those of the old frontiersmen can for the most part trace their ancestry in design back to the ancient scramasax, dagger, dirk, and the Bowie. Modern throwing-knives come in both professional and sporting styles with some being made to throw only by the blade and others made to be hurled by the handle. The ones in greatest demand by the average sportsman knife-thrower are the latter—and the Bowie style is the most popular hunting type. Both deer and

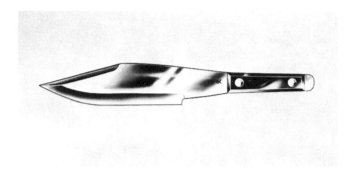

21. The Tru-Bal Bowie-Axe throwing-knife.

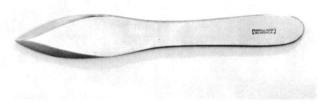

22. The famous Randall-Made throwing-knife.

vicious wild boar are among big game animals having been killed with such a blade.

A wedding of sorts was performed by this writer in January 1959 with the idea of combining the Bowie knife design and the scramasax pattern into an all-purpose throwing, hunting, camping, and survival knife. This helped start a surge of interest in knife throwing in the early 1960s, primarily among devotees of black-powder shooting—the muzzleloaders.

Over the several following decades, the Tru-Bal Bowie-Axe, as it is called, made knife throwing history—especially among the American black-powder knife-throwers, big game hunters, and those who just chop with it as a camp tool. It was a favorite, too, of many servicemen fighting in the Vietnam War, and was the basis for the dozen or so throwing patterns designed over the years that helped get the sport off the ground.

As pointed out in the first chapter, a good throwing-knife should have three basic features: proper balance for throwing, a length long enough for control, and enough weight for good, solid penetration of the target wood. Designs can vary considerably, but a good throwing-knife *must* have these three characteristics.

Designs have indeed varied considerably, but in spite of its diversity, the throwing-knife, through the long history of its development, has won many an enthusiast who marveled at its designs, loved holding it ready for the throw, and naturally reveled in the pleasure of striking a target squarely, and point first. That is why it has been, and is still now, one of the most gratifying and enjoyable recreational sports you will ever find.

IV
The Art of
the Professionals

HOLLYWOOD, CALIFORNIA is merely one town
amid a myriad of other communities that is known
as the Greater Los Angeles Trading Area. It has
long been associated with show-business glitter and
glamour. The very word "Hollywood" has a special
meaning of its own—not only for the rank and
file of movie and television fans—but also for the
star performers in every field of entertainment.
This includes many of the great professional knife
throwers of the 20th century.

Southern California, because of its excellent year-
round climate and numerous motion picture studios
is (and has always been) the home of many super
performers using knives, tomahawks, guns, ropes,
and whips. Among their ranks are the late Frank
Dean, the great Carl Pitti, the fabulous Skeeter
Vaughan, Larry Cisewski, the wonderful team of

Sylvester and Barbara Braun, and many more—some who are still living and some who rightly became legends in their own lifetime.

Knife throwing as a sport, art, science, and profession owes a great deal to one outstanding professional in particular—the late Frank Dean. The story of this amazingly talented showman should be an inspiration to any sportsman who has had the pleasure of hitting his target with a throwing-knife!

Frank Dean

As a knife thrower, Frank Dean was as much an expert as any professional could ever be. His untimely passing away in January, 1985, just a few weeks short of his 77th birthday, greatly saddened his many friends; Will Rogers, Jr. especially was grieved, since, as a young man, Frank Dean had been a close friend and the rope-spinning protégé of the world-renowned Will Rogers, Sr.

Frank Dean achieved his greatest fame as a world-champion cowboy roper, rope twirler, sharp shooter, whip snapper, and trick horseman who, in the company of his wife, Bernice (who was herself a famous roper and equestrian), often entertained audiences by doing headstands on horseback! He established a number of world records with ropes and whips, including those which were earned for his 80 foot-long whip snapping and his unique ability to twirl or spin 15 ropes at one time. Appropriately, he often was called the "Dean" of trick ropers.

As a small boy, Frank learned the use of ropes—how to spin and throw them for his great horse "catches" later as a performer. He also developed considerable skill as a knife thrower. For a high-school graduation stunt, he performed by throwing knives around a classmate who was concealed against the target boards by a screen of newspapers. Even in his early teens when he had not yet finished his high-school education, Frank had done shows professionally.

In the late 1920s, Frank worked the rodeo circuits doing all his various stunts with ropes, whips, horses, trick shooting, and knives. In 1928, he joined with the Sells Floto Circus and Buffalo Bill's Wild West Show, his first circus appearances. A year later he joined the Al G. Barnes Circus and worked with two of the greatest professionals in knife throwing at the time—Bennie Pete Pitti and Frank Chicarello. At this time, he was still only 21.

Every professional knife thrower, along with performing the more or less standard stunts that make up most of the act, usually has one trick which is uniquely his own. In 1934, Frank Dean became a specialist in the art of throwing big, heavy 16-inch meat cleavers. A year later, while working in a Wild West show at the 1935 Yokohama Exposition in Japan, he married a lovely young lady who not only was a stunt woman and performed with ropes and horses in the show, but also acted as his assistant in the knife throwing and meat-cleaver act. Incidentally, the marriage ceremony was performed while they were both on horseback! She was the beautiful Bernice Hoppe, and for years after their marriage, Frank's friends would joke with him about it, saying, "Frank, you took advantage of your wife when you got her to marry you."

"What do you mean, I took advantage of her?" Frank would retort.

"Because," his friends would say, "how could any girl say 'no' to you while you were throwing knives around her every day and asking her to marry you at the same time!"

It took a full year before Bernice could feel comfortable about the "thud" made by the heavy meat cleavers as they smashed into the boards around her. But in all his more than 50 years as a professional knife thrower, Frank Dean never drew a single drop of blood from his assistant due to a bad throw. He often explained to an audience that his lovely wife standing there was never the "target." Only the boards around her into which he hurled the 16-inch knives and cleavers were the "target."

Over many years Frank and Bernice Dean worked in shows all over the world—both before and after World War II. During the war, Frank served as a sergeant of artillery overseas in Europe for several years, but when he returned, he and Bernice just picked up the act where they had left off.

In 1937, Frank Dean wrote and published a small 24-page booklet called *The Art of Knife Throwing*.

In it he explained many of the secrets and tricks of professional knife throwing; also included were a number of interesting line drawings and some photos. This book, for the first time in the history of the art, gave many sportsmen knife-throwers some very basic information and the encouragement to take up knife throwing—as a hobby, at least.

This was also a period in his career when he appeared in numerous motion pictures performing with ropes and throwing-knives, and doing stunts on horseback. He worked in the movies with a number of other famous knife throwers—especially with his great friend, Jack Cavanaugh. One of the stunts they performed together was a "knife throwers' battle" in which they each threw knives into a wooden shield held by the other. (The same type of stunt is still used by one of the world's greatest knife throwers, the incomparable Fritz Brumback of West Germany.)

Frank Dean had a great collection of stories and incidents which he would enjoy telling to friends. One happened during a tour he made of Japan when he was using a folding knife-board that had the split running down the center. Before Bernice took her place against it, Frank would throw a couple of knives at the center to warm up. On one occasion, when two Japanese stage workers brought out the big folding board, they got behind it to stay out of sight during the knife-throwing sequence. Frank threw the practice knife to get the range, and the

23. Frank Dean standing against Skeeter Vaughan's target board. Notice resemblance to Frank's boyhood idol, Will Rogers.

blade went right through the narrow split at the fold, stopping only when the hilt hit the boards. It greatly frightened the two hidden helpers, but fortunately for all concerned, the blade had come through the target between them and just missed both of them!

Over his long career, Frank Dean always considered himself a historian of the cowboy arts of roping, whip snapping, rope spinning, and horsemanship. He was a talented writer and the author of a number of excellent books, including *Trick and Fancy Riding,* and *Will Rogers' Rope Tricks,* plus an instruction book explaining dozens of his stunts with ropes. Frank's most famous book was called *Cowboy Fun.* Actually, this was only the first half of a projected two-book set, and the second book was just about completed at the time of his death.

Frank Dean and his wife, Bernice, worked shows in many different countries with their performance called "Western Acts in Modern Splendor." As one of the foremost ropers and rope spinners of his generation, he left a great legacy to his friends when, in 1980, he organized the International Trick and Fancy Ropers Association which, at the time of this writing, has some 300 members from ten different countries.

It was a terrible blow to him when Bernice died in his arms that same year. Five years later, he too became a legend. He was a good friend not only to the author, but to his many associates and peers in the entertainment business. He was very modest about his own accomplishments, but was lavish in his praise for other artists with ropes, whips, and knives. In a letter to me, he once wrote that Skeeter Vaughan was the most consistently accurate knife thrower he had ever known. Skeeter—like Frank—

24. Frank Dean's personal throwing-knives.

in a lifetime of knife and tomahawk throwing had *never* drawn blood because of a bad throw from any assistant who worked with him.

As mentioned, Frank Dean devoted much of his time and knowledge to helping other artists who worked with horses, ropes, whips, and knives to strive for perfection. To knife throwers in general, professional and sportsmen alike, he left one very important suggestion. Writing these following words to live by—or throw by—to his friend in England, Mr. Ivan L. Thurlow, he wrote: "A final bit of advice. Never throw *at* a human target—throw *around* it. They last longer that way."

The Art of Impalement: The Performers

Cowboy Fun is a pictorial history which covers many phases of cowboy entertainment, including roping, fast draw, gun spinning, fancy shooting, whip popping, rodeo clowns, and various cowboy tricks. It has one additional section which is devoted entirely to knife and edged-weapon throwing, and it is this last section of this fine book which is of special interest to knife-throwing enthusiasts. Frank knew a vast deal about—and most of them personally—the great knife throwers of the 20th century, and this is something that is quite apparent in the book.

One of the amazing performers Frank describes in his book is the great Argentine thrower, Adolfo Rossi, who had a rare technique of throwing a knife, wrapped for half its length with wool yarn, in such a way that the padded part would strike the assistant's arm or shoulder with the blade almost straight up. It would then roll over and stick into the target. Rossi would first practice hitting balloons with the padded blades—bouncing them into the wood without breaking the balloons! For the climax of his act he would split an apple or potato on the back of his wife's neck with a razor-sharp machete, but eventually he gave up this dangerous stunt because it was too unnerving to an audience.

Some stunts in the "impalement arts" seem more dangerous than they really are. The great Joe Gibson and his wife Hannah once had a sequence in their act in which he threw big two-pound hatchets around his wife. Since a full-spin hatchet throw requires more throwing distance than does the fast half-spin knife throw used by many pros, it can appear to be more dangerous. Mrs. Gibson, after watching the audience react very nervously to the stunt one night, told Joe she thought they should scrub the big hatchets from the act (which they did).

Another note about the Gibsons, who originally performed in Europe, is the fact that they can be credited for first bringing the now famous "Wheel of Death" to the United States in 1938. The "Wheel of Death" is a circular knife-board, about six feet in diameter and two inches thick. It is constructed from a softwood that will hold the blades well— usually sugar pine or white pine. It is mounted on a metal or sturdy wooden stand with a ball bearing arrangement in the center so the board can be spun fairly rapidly—even up to 120 RPM.

There is a step for the assistant to stand on, along with handle grips and sometimes a shoulder restraint to keep her steady while the wheel revolves. The knives are thrown rapidly around her as she spins, fencing her in. This act takes a lot of practice, but is not as dangerous as it might appear—unless the thrower does the act blindfolded, as Joe Gibson used to do. Joe mainly relied on hearing a click as his wife passed the vertical position, but perhaps he could also "see a little." Who knows?

Today the "Wheel of Death" is used by almost every professional knife thrower in the business. One variation involves flaming knives, thrown fast by the blades with the handles wrapped and soaked in a flammable material that causes it to burn most dramatically!

Another unbelievable variation involved one of Frank Dean's best friends and old movie stunt partner, Jack Cavanaugh. Jack was considered to be one of the very best throwers in the business— he was perhaps the only one who could actually stand on his head and throw knives all around his wife while she spun on a revolving "Wheel of Death." It was one of the most amazing stunts in the history of professional knife throwing.

In *Cowboy Fun,* Frank Dean tells about many other amazing stunts, including a famous armless knife thrower named Paul Des Muke who, in the 1930s while working as a featured performer with Ringling Bros. and Barnum & Bailey Circus, threw knives expertly with his feet while sitting in a straight-backed chair. Also described is the amazing act of the "Great Collins," who threw knives while balanced on a slack wire, and the "Riding Hobsons," who dressed as Indians and threw knives from horseback at a full gallop. Another team, the Parkos, threw from a rolla-rolla board, which is about as unstable a platform as you can get.

Another great act featured in Dean's book was Tex Orton, who had one spectacular throwing stunt

25. Paul LaCross in action with the "Wheel of Death." His assistant is spinning at 120 RPM.

that involved splitting an apple resting on his wife's neck while she bent over backwards. He also liked to throw two knives at once, simultaneously cutting two strips of paper held out by his wife, Alice. This same act is also performed by Paul LaCrosse.

Over a period of more than five decades, Frank Dean appeared on shows with many of the other great knife throwers. Two of his very good friends were "Bennie Pete" Pitti, and Ben's talented son, Carl Pitti. Bennie Pete was a very close friend of two

26. The knife that "shoots."

famous stars of the 1920s—Tom Mix, the cowboy movie actor, and Will Rogers. All three were ropers and rope spinners of the first rank, but Bennie Pete was probably the best-known professional knife thrower of that era, as well as being a master with whips and ropes.

Ben's son, Carl Pitti, became a Hollywood stunt man, as well as a partner in later years with his father in many of their great acts involving horses, knives, ropes, and bows and arrows. Frank Dean once said that in his opinion Carl Pitti was the best he had ever seen for all-around coordination with arrows, guns, and knives. It was Ben Pitti who invented the "knife that shoots." This was a knife with a weighted metal-slider firing pin fitted into a slot in the blade. A short, blank-cartridge chambered barrel was welded in the slot, and aligned with the sliding bar firing pin. A screw on one side would adjust the tension, so that when the thrown knife hit the target boards, the firing pin slider would bang into the blank cartridge causing a loud explosion—a fitting finale to the fine act. Both Bennie Pete and Carl Pitti used this device for many years, as does Larry Cisewski, an excellent West Coast thrower currently active.

Two other great friends of Frank Dean were Sylvester and Barbara Braun, who are still performing their act called "Wizards of the West." The Brauns present a great show involving trick riding, whips, ropes, throwing-knives, and hatchets. They were married in 1952, and like the Deans before them, were both circus performers. Working in the Clyde Beatty Railroad Circus when they met, she and Sylvester were ropers and riders, while Bennie Pete was the circus knife-thrower. Although the younger man had been throwing knives professionally since the 1940s, Ben showed Sylvester many of the knife throwing stunts he used. Another great knife thrower, Frank Mansfield, also taught Sylvester much about "the impalement arts"; however, it was the 1937 edition of Frank Dean's book that really got him started in the business. Although he usually throws 10 knives fast and close with the half-spin using the blade grip, Sylvester Braun also throws the full spin with both knives and hatchets. He has also used the "Wheel of Death" in the act, but his lovely wife, Barbara, even though she didn't mind having the knives thrown all around her, hated the upside-down sensation of the spinning boards.

Sylvester liked to start his act with four knives thrown into the board—two while facing the target and two thrown backward between his legs. Then Barbara would stand up against the board and he would build the usual "ladder"—five to a side. Like all "pros" who work with an assistant, the knives are always thrown from the bottom up, so that there is no danger of a spinning knife striking one previously thrown above it.

In a letter to this writer, Sylvester once wrote: "We do a number of stunts in the act, but one incident of an accidental nature is worth telling. We were working in a shopping mall some years ago and I threw a knife at a balloon which Barbara was holding. I guess the knife hit the balloon with the flat side because instead of breaking the balloon, it bounced the knife back into my hand. As I caught it, I instantly hurled it back again and this time broke the balloon. It was a trick, alas, I could not repeat."

There are and were many other talented professional knife throwers who were outstanding in their accomplishments, and the list of names mentioned herein is a "Who's Who" of the 20th century's greatest artists who demonstrated the "art of impalement." These include the great Indian throwers like Steve Clemento, Lawrence Pierce (Chief White Cloud of the Senecas), and his son Kenneth Pierce ("Che Che"), who carries on the famous White Cloud name and knife-throwing act with his wife, Donna. (Donna, incidentally, is a descendant of the fabled Daniel Boone.) Also, there is Augie Gomez,

27. The stars of the "Wizards of the West," Sylvester and Barbara Braun.

28. Kenneth Pierce showing his classic professional stance.

Rodd Redwing, and the celebrated Cherokee actor, stuntman, and knife thrower who is acknowledged to be the world's greatest tomahawk thrower—Grey Otter, otherwise known as George E. (Skeeter) Vaughan. More about him later.

Other notable throwers include Al Cody and also the Shooting Mansfields, who doubled as the "The Yukons" in a very good impalement act. There are celebrated throwers in Europe too, like the great Toranados and the fine British performers Stan

Brion, Ivan L. Thurlow, and R. M. Fearnley. The best this author has ever seen working on a television show is Fritz Brumbach, the great West German performer. He throws very fast and too close for comfort sometimes—or so it seems. Brumbach is an amazing artist with knives, including giant Gurkha knives, whips, and battle-axes, and like other throwers, often works with flaming knives. This is fine for an indoor act, but if done outdoors on a windy day it can create quite a bit of discomfort for the assistant.

Special mention should be made of Paul LaCross, who truly has become a legend in his own time. Often billed as "the world's greatest" in the stunts he does so well, Paul LaCross has performed amazing feats with revolvers, rifles, lumberman long-handled axes, bow and arrows, and best of all, his 16-inch throwing-knives and small throwing-hatchets. His left-handed style of throwing is unique.

The following is a fascinating insight Paul LaCross gives regarding his stunts with the knives. Paul writes, "For sport throwing, I like a heavier knife than one used for stage work with a girl assistant. The lighter knife can be thrown faster and peeled off the hand more quickly. When you hold a dozen knives fanned out in one hand like I do, a better job of fanning and peeling from one hand to another can be done more easily with a slightly lighter knife. Also, when I throw two knives at a time from one hand, the combined weight of the two knives should

29. The great left-handed knife thrower, Paul LaCross.

not be much heavier than just one used for hunting or muzzleloading competitions where the thrower often has a heavy knife to match the weight of his tomahawk."

Paul LaCross uses a matched set of knives (made for him by this writer) which are 16 inches overall and weigh 15 ounces. Larry Cisewski and John Lepiarz, who are both outstanding professionals, also have adopted the Paul LaCross throwing-knife for use in their acts. Many professionals seem to prefer a long knife, from 15 to 16 inches in overall length with a weight not exceeding 15 ounces. The big wide knives are usually only $\frac{1}{8}$ inch thick, allowing easy penetration of the target boards. The "pros" like them because a large blade has more glitter and flash than the smaller models used by some performers for very fast, short-range blade throws.

Not all professionals use the blade throw. Frank Dean was always a handle thrower, as is Larry Cisewski. Fritz Brumbach does all his long throws with the handle grip—and if the famed Gurkha knife of India is used, the design of the weapon makes it throwable only by the handle.

A number of lesser-known knife throwers have emerged in the 1970s and '80s, including magician Joe Eddy Fairchild and his brother Bob, Jay Evans, Stewart Lipke, Al Lamarre, Dick Haines, Jerome Smith and a few others who are active in the business. All these younger professionals are doing well and have great talent.

There are also a few sportsmen knife-throwers who are good enough to turn pro. One is Arnold R. Sandubrae of Palm Springs, California, and another is Lewis Brotherton of Florida. Lewis is a retired Marine Master Sergeant who was a member for some years of the U.S. Marine rifle and pistol teams. What

30. Dick Haines outlines his assistant with the fast half-spin throw.

he can do throwing a triple and even a quadruple spin with a Bowie-Axe throwing-knife is unbelievable!

Lew Brotherton learned about the art of knife throwing as a boy, but in the Marines he was taught the blade throw "shift." The way the blade is gripped enables the thrower either to speed up or slow down the rate of spin, depending on the distance to the target. By gripping the blade an inch or so above your normal grip and more toward the overall center of the knife, you can slow the spin and stick the target at a slightly greater distance. By gripping the tip of the blade at its extreme point, without that inch or so protruding from beneath your bottom finger, you can speed up the spin, and stick the blade at a slightly shorter distance than would be normal for your style of blade throwing.

As in the case of Lew Brotherton this blade throw "shift" was especially good when hurling a bayonet in a combat situation. This method is not too practical with a knife thrown by the handle, but it does work sometimes for blade throws. Even professionals who throw by the blade can easily make such an adjustment for distance if necessary.

Some noted professionals are famous for special skills not necessarily connected with knife or tomahawk throwing. Paul LaCross, for instance, has become world famous for his rifle and revolver marksmanship, his fast draw artistry, and also his remarkable skill as a trick-shot artist with the bow and arrow. Many other famous pros do tricks with ropes or whips, and perform stunts on horseback, while throwing knives at the same time.

Those with amazing balancing skills enabling them to perform knife and tomahawk throwing feats on a slack wire (like the "Great Collins" before World War II) can add interest to their act by including a balancing stunt. A good example is "The Great LaMar," otherwise known as Al Lamarre, who has achieved considerable fame as an aerialist with exceptional balancing skills. Using a stage name of Chief Golden Eagle, Lamarre often performs his

31. Larry Cisewski practicing his backward throw.

knife and tomahawk throwing stunts while balanced on a rolla-rolla board, the unusual stance and platform made famous by the celebrated Parkos of an earlier era. Al Lamarre, decked out in an Indian costume, is carrying on the Parkos tradition, using knives crafted for him by the author.

Another knife-throwing stunt, perfected by Larry Cisewski, is the "Devil's Doorway." This contraption features a heavy board door which revolves rapidly within a frame while the assistant is secured to one side of it. The thrower has to time his throws so that the blades will stick in the back side of the door as it spins. This is an interesting variation of the "Wheel of Death"—and it is indeed quite spectacular.

One great European thrower mentioned earlier is Fritz Brumbach, who does a stunt once performed by Frank Dean on a movie set. With great speed he rapidly throws a series of knives into a pair of wooden shields held up by his assistant. His speed, which equals that of Kenneth Pierce (Che Che) of the famed White Cloud family, is so great that the assistant almost staggers under a series of knife impacts, much like fast hammer blows, hitting the shields she carries as she dances about.

Another talented knife thrower is magician Joe Eddy Fairchild, who combines the "Wheel of Death" knife-throwing stunt with his magic act. His assistant, in this case his wife Betty, steps up against the big revolving board and is covered from head to toe by a large circular paper screen. Joe Eddy then gives the wheel a mighty spin, steps back, and hurls a half-dozen knives in rapid succession into the fast turning target boards, with the final one hitting directly in the center! This usually creates a stir of apprehension among the spectators, but Joe Eddy then runs to the front of the stage and opens a large box or trunk—out of which steps Betty, to the wonderment of the audience.

Over the years there have been many innovations connected with the "arts of impalement," some of which Frank Dean has described as being among the most celebrated stunts found anywhere. Every professional performer with knives and tomahawks has no doubt explored all the standard tricks of the trade, but they all constantly look for new and different types of stunts to provide special thrills for their audiences. We wish them all the best of luck!

The Lady Assistants

One of the amazing things about the "art of impalement" which puzzles many people who witness these knife or tomahawk throwing acts, involves this question: "How does that pretty girl have the courage to stand against the target boards while the weapons are hurled into the wood so close to her?" Since a team of two people must make up the act, much credit for the success of a knife thrower's performance depends upon his lovely assistant. In many of the great teams of both past and present, the thrower and his assistant are man and wife.

There is no doubt that it takes considerable courage—especially at first when the act is just breaking in, so to speak—for a lady to expose herself to what appears to be deadly danger. It does take awhile to get used to the ominous "thud" as the knives or 'hawks penetrate the wood. To prepare for such an act, these brave ladies first get used to the sound by having the thrower hurl his weapons quite wide of her body as she stands about six inches in front of the boards. Only when she has complete confidence in the skill of the thrower is she ready to work up a routine of stunts that appear dangerous—and could really be so, were it not for the prowess of the "pro" and his set of perfectly matched throwing-knives.

Lovely ladies like Bernice Dean, Hannah Gibson, Barbara Braun, Marie Mansfield, Alice Orton, Donna Pierce, and the wife and daughter of Paul LaCross, have all made the throwers look very good because of their own coolness, calm, and beauty "under fire." Without a pretty lady standing there against the boards in a colorful costume, the act would not be nearly as exciting and spectacular for the audience.

The lady standing there throughout each phase of the entire performance has trained herself to remain not only perfectly still as the knives crash into the wood all around her, but actually to think of other things and practically ignore the sound and fury so close to her vulnerable frame. As for the throwers themselves, they are the most careful and skillful of men in their chosen profession. The concentration they must put forth while making those fast and close throws has got to be 100 percent!

Skeeter Vaughan has explained his thoughts as his act is about to begin. "I simply block the girl out of my mind when I throw. To me, she suddenly does not exist. I simply use her silhouette as a focal point and concentrate all my powers on hitting the exact spot on the board I throw at." He knows, of course,

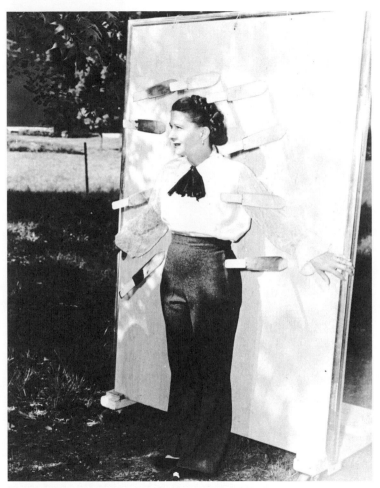

32. The lovely Marie Mansfield, who with her husband Frank, made up "The Yukons." Their act flourished from the 1930s into the 1950s.

that the girl is there—maybe holding a strip of paper in her mouth for him to chop off with a tomahawk or knife—but he is so intent on hitting his target that the girl might as well be sitting in the audience instead of standing before him. He prays a lot to the Great Spirit to make his aim true, and this same mental attitude is just about identical with all professional knife throwers who work with a lovely assistant.

Accidents are, unfortunately, reported from time to time. One that shows the stamina of the assistant involved a thrower accidentally sticking a knife into the upper right arm of his assistant on a MGM movie set. The next morning, however, she was back on the set, briskly rubbing her left arm. Asked why she was rubbing the left arm instead of the injured right one, she replied, "The right arm doesn't hurt—it's my left arm where they gave me that damn tetanus shot!"

The great professionals, past and present, owe much to the beauty, talent, and courage of the ladies who make their impalement acts so interesting. A very special word of thanks is due to those ladies—one and all!

V

The Saga
of Skeeter Vaughan

THE GUNS WERE silent as sounds of intermittent shelling faded away in the distance. There was no moonlight, but the night skies were clear and full of stars, and what light there was reflected off the mantle of newly fallen snow. Visibility was quite good, considering the darkness of this late November night in 1944, and the blackish object in the distance could be seen clearly against the snow.

That dark object was a German sentry, on guard duty beside a bunker complex which included a Nazi pillbox that had held up the American advance all day and was giving the U.S. Infantry considerable resistance.

The six-man patrol of the U.S. Moccasin Rangers—all American Indians especially gifted with "night sight"—was commanded by Sergeant George E. Vaughan, nicknamed "Skeeter." At the moment, the squad was belly down in the snow behind the German bunker complex, concealed some 35 yards away in a small stand of timber on the brow of the hill.

The sentry had his back to the hill and stood facing the American lines. He was at least ninety feet downhill from where the Indian G.I.'s lay in the snow assessing the situation.

The six-man patrol had silently filtered through the German lines and circled behind the bunker-pillbox fortress. Their mission was to take out the pillbox by eliminating the garrison, and to accomplish the job before dawn when the Allied advance was to resume. A great many American lives depended upon the success of this mission.

The problem at the moment was to eliminate the sentry and to do it silently. It would be easy to shoot the soldier, but the crack of a rifle shot would alert the Germans and make this important assignment a costly, if not an impossible, one. It would also be very difficult to creep down from the timber line and knife the sentry, since it was all open ground between them. Furthermore, since the German seemed quite alert, an assailant might be quickly spotted approaching against the light background of new snow.

There was a slight chance that the problem could be solved by the commander of the patrol, a full-blooded Cherokee Indian from California named Skeeter Vaughan. He was only one month away from his 22nd birthday, an event he might never celebrate if his plan failed to succeed.

As a boy, Skeeter Vaughan had lived in numerous places, including Indian reservations in California, Oregon, and other parts of the West. His formal education was interrupted many times, but he finally graduated in 1939 from high school in Alhambra, California. His practical education, however, started when he was only eight years old under the tutelage of his grandfather, Old Limping Bear, a Tennessee-born Cherokee originally from the Smoky Mountains. This education dealt mostly with a large range of weapons including rifles, revolvers, and pistols, with special emphasis placed on knives and tomahawks. Considerable time was also devoted to the handling of whips for driving mules and horses, along with the use of ropes for basic ranch work.

All these things Skeeter mastered with skill and expertise, but he developed a special affinity for knives and tomahawks and the art of throwing them. He became so proficient with these two weapons that, even as a teenager, he was able to turn professional and receive pay for his performances as a knife and tomahawk thrower in carnivals and wild west shows.

When he was only 12 years old, Skeeter killed a pronghorn antelope with a thrown knife (with some help from Old Limping Bear, who sort of "flagged" it in Skeeter's direction). As a youth on the Umatilla Indian reservation in Oregon during the 1930s, his desire to achieve perfection in throwing knives and tomahawks was partly economic. This was because the Great Depression was in full swing and rifle ammunition cost a dime a shell, a costly sum with cash being so scarce at the time. So when hunting wild game, an activity that made up an important part of the family's food supply in those years, Skeeter seldom used a gun except on very big game such as deer, bear, or elk. Still, he treasured those rare occasions when a deer was downed with a thrown knife. On one occasion he even killed a grouse with a thrown tomahawk. We should note that he is considered to be the first modern-day thrower to bring down big game with a throwing-knife.

During those formative years while growing up, Skeeter Vaughan worked on ranches in various states in the West—a boy doing a man's work as a cowboy and horsebreaker. He also did stints with several rodeos as a performer and one year worked in "Doc Willetson's Big Medicine Show" as it toured the West, throwing his tomahawks and 16-inch-long knives made from old British bayonets.

In 1942, when he was 19, he enlisted in the U.S. Cavalry, taking his basic training at the historic camp at Fort Riley, Kansas. He was soon elevated to the position of a full-time instructor. Besides teaching recruits the use of weapons, he also trained them in unarmed combat—a field in which he was considered an expert, despite his being of just a medium build and standing only five feet eight inches in his combat boots.

He reached the rank of sergeant during his two years at Fort Riley, during which time he taught literally thousands of recruits the basics of weaponry, from handguns, rifles, and carbines, to machine guns and the 37 mm cannon. He was later transferred to the 18th Recon. Squadron at Fort Lewis, Washington, and soon afterward ended up in England in the spring of 1944. Two days after D-Day, he landed with his unit on Omaha Beach in Normandy, as part of the Allied invasion forces.

It was about two weeks later that the unit of Indians called the Moccasin Rangers was organized. This was a very elite group of 15 men, all of whom were well trained and blessed with "night sight." It was organized for night patrols and reconnaissance work against the Germans and usually operated behind enemy lines. The exploits of this special unit soon became well-known, for it was a force that the Nazis found difficult to deal with.

Tonight, however, Skeeter Vaughan and his patrol lay in the snow in the midst of the German army's fabled Siegfried Line, and the bunker and pillbox below were a part of that vast network of barriers to the Allied advance.

"What are we gonna do, Sarge?" asked a G.I.

Skeeter shook his head silently, his eyes intent on the back of the sentry 30 yards away.

"Could you throw your knife that far and nail him? We're gonna have to try something," the G.I. insisted.

"O.K.," said Sgt. Vaughan. "But even for a pro, that's one hell of a long throw—and all downhill too! If I miss, you guys better be ready to blast him, just in case."

He drew the weapon from its sheath and held it by the blade. It was a customized knife he had made from a bayonet—16 inches in overall length and exactly the type of throwing-knife he had used most of his life, on and off the stage.

It was now or never!

Quietly Skeeter crawled out of the timber as far as he dared and stood up. The back of the sentry was still toward him. Now Skeeter was in the open, silently praying that he had been unobserved.

With a skill developed over many years of continual practice, Skeeter hurled his bayonet knife in a high trajectory, aiming for a spot about three feet above the head of the sentry. The weapon turned silently over and over in its long downhill pinwheel flight, and to Skeeter's amazement, the sentry dropped face down into the snow without a sound—the weapon had penetrated the sentry's head at the base of his skull. Had Skeeter missed, or only slightly wounded the sentry, his Moccasin Ranger team would have had to open up with rifles or automatic fire, thus alerting the pillbox. The entire mission might then have been a failure.

As the result of Skeeter's miraculous throw, however, the patrol was able to reach the back door of the pillbox unobserved. They knocked gently on the door and the German soldiers inside, thinking their relief had arrived, opened up—and were quickly eliminated by the Moccasin Rangers.

The next day, the Americans advanced further into Germany, and members of Skeeter's unit, checking tracks in the snow, measured Skeeter's life-and-death knife throw at 87 feet—downhill and in the dark. Considering the distance thrown, Skeeter had probably made the longest successful throw in the annals of knife throwing, thereby adding another exploit to the legend of this fine Cherokee Indian who is now recognized by his peers as the world's greatest professional tomahawk thrower and the equal of any knife thrower in the business.

As the war went on, Skeeter and his Moccasin Rangers were involved in numerous exploits that made them heroes among the American troops. Unfortunately, one by one, these extremely dangerous missions killed off his Indian friends, and by the end of the war, Skeeter was the only surviving member of the original team of Moccasin Rangers. Skeeter himself was wounded five times in battle, including a nearly fatal head wound.

After taking part in the famed December 1944 Battle of the Bulge, Skeeter wound up in an army hospital in Winchester, England. He was hospitalized with a bad case of "trench foot," caused by constantly having wet feet from the snow and cold.

This medical problem, also called "immersion foot," had a major adverse influence upon the troops of all nations during the First World War, and although improvements were made in the Second World War, it still remained a serious problem. The lack of circulation in the feet due to constant cold temperatures and wet boots often made amputation of the victim's feet a necessity.

This was almost true in Skeeter's case. The doctor at Winchester told him that his feet would have to be amputated because of the extreme seriousness of his condition. Skeeter, however, had other ideas, for he was determined that he would die before he'd let them cut off his feet and ship him home as a helpless, and hopeless cripple. Along with his career as a professional knife and tomahawk thrower, he had worked as a rodeo performer. Also, breaking in horses, before the war, was part of Skeeter's life's blood. But looking at his small feet, now swollen so much, it seemed that amputation was the only answer. So, Skeeter stole a pair of size 10½ boots, worked them on over his normally size 6½ swollen feet, and then simply walked away from the hospital, AWOL.

With luck, Skeeter managed to bum his way down to Southampton, a port of embarkation for American troops headed for the front. Because there was no way that he'd be able to rejoin his unit without official help, he turned himself in to the provost marshall and told the officer the complete story. He pointed out that he would much rather be killed in battle than have his feet amputated, which would leave him unable to put his own feet in a pair of stirrups and ride a horse.

The provost marshall told Skeeter that he was the first G.I. in the European theater of war who really *wanted* to get back to the fighting at the front. So he made an exception, and Skeeter was finally shipped across to his own unit—bad feet and all. Miraculously he recovered, in spite of being on active duty. To this day, however, his feet are still so tender that he cannot wear anything but Indian moccasins. He often jokes that the soles of his feet are so sensitive that even through a moccasin he can "step on an ice cream cone and tell the flavor!"

Through the various replacement depots, he finally reached his unit, now joined with the 9th Armoured Division, just in time to reach the fabled bridge at Remagen. His outfit located it first, and when the 9th Armour secured it, Skeeter was one of the first to cross over.

Wounded five times, and appropriately well decorated, Skeeter turned down a battlefield commission, preferring his role as sergeant. After the war, the army kept him from being discharged for several months because of his specialized knowledge and teaching qualifications. It seems the army wanted him to teach a new group of servicemen combat and command techniques before allowing him to don his buckskins and head back to California. He was discharged on his 23rd birthday—his great birthday gift from a grateful Uncle Sam!

33. Skeeter Vaughan practicing with his 16-inch bayonet throwing-knives.

Skeeter had lost his only brother during the war, killed in action while serving as a tail gunner in the 8th Air Force. Now only his mother and stepfather were home in L.A., and that's where Skeeter headed to start life again as a newborn civilian.

After getting married and starting a family, Skeeter decided to forgo his knife and tomahawk career since his wife was not enthusiastic about his career as a showman. He entered the booming construction business as a cement contractor and did his knife and tomahawk act as a sideline occupation. He also found part-time work in motion pictures and appeared in countless movies as a bit player, a knife thrower, and quite often as a stunt

34. Skeeter Vaughan's bayonet knife and stainless steel tomahawk.

man. He later performed in numerous television series such as "Gunsmoke," and for years was in demand for television commercials as well.

For about 20 years he remained fairly busy in the construction business, but it became more of a side-line as his fame grew and the entertainment industry began to absorb most of his time. Since 1959, he has performed all over the world with knives and tomahawks and as an actor and stunt man. The list is almost endless, and he has even been inducted into the "Stuntman's Hall of Fame." It is said that he has thrown his knives and tomahawks around more famous celebrities in the movie and television entertainment world than any other professional in the field. And never, *never* has he even scratched any person who volunteered to act as his assistant and stand against the boards.

The knives Skeeter uses while performing are ones he made himself from old English bayonets of good Sheffield steel dating back to the 1860s. He throws an even dozen in his act with handles formed of leather and covered with buckskin. All are perfectly matched, 16-inch knives that he throws by the point grip for a long, fast, half-spin throw. His "pinchgrip" style is unique among the professionals of the present day, but it works well for him. With this grip, he demonstrates an uncanny accuracy which no other pro thrower has ever been able to surpass.

Skeeter also uses a pipe tomahawk with a configuration that is his own special design. The leading edge, or upper right-hand corner of the blade, is raised for maximum penetration and the weapon is beautifully balanced to perfect Skeeter's precision throwing.

Not just involved in the entertainment business, Skeeter, whose Cherokee name is Grey Otter, has done much to help his fellow American Indians. He served on the board of directors of the American Indian Scholarship Fund, which enables Indian students to continue their college education in California. He was also a council member of the Los Angeles Indian Center, and as a Chief of the Federated Indian Tribes (or Indian Nations) for three years, Skeeter proudly wears, while in costume, his symbolic red feather—the Indian badge of honor for having been wounded in battle.

And finally, a note on the nickname "Skeeter" to close our saga of this great man. His now famous nickname was received when he was just a youngster when, although only 12, he was doing a man's work of bucking and falling timber in an Oregon lumber camp. One payday, the camp foreman held back a $10 bill that the boy had earned, taunted him, and told Skeeter to come and take it from him if he was man enough. The lad really needed that money.

Compared to the foreman, who was a big husky man weighing perhaps 225 pounds, Skeeter was a skinny kid, about five feet tall and around 110 pounds in weight. Skeeter started to walk away from the foreman, but after a few steps he stopped, pulled out his long throwing-knife from his belt, turned and threw it so that it passed within an inch or two of the foreman's ear. The knife stuck in a tree just behind him.

As the foreman reached behind him to withdraw the knife, Skeeter pulled another blade from his boot and waited. Suddenly the big man, pale-faced and shaky, took out his wallet, threw a $10 bill on the ground before him and walked away.

One of the lumberjacks who had witnessed the entire episode, proclaimed loudly to the group gathering around the boy: "For a little 'skeeter, he sure carries a big stinger!" And, of course, the nickname stuck!

35. The legendary "Grey Otter."

VI
Tomahawk Throwing

THE STALWART Indian swept his arm forward and the glittering tomahawk spun from his hand, whirled through the air, and thudded into the target board scant inches from the girl's pretty face. The strip of folded white paper jutting out from between her lips had been cleanly severed in half and the chopped-off piece fluttered gently to the floor of the stage.

A prolonged burst of applause swelled from the audience and Grey Otter, a celebrated member of the Cherokee Indian Nation, smiled and waved his arms in acknowledgment. His lovely assistant also bowed in response to the thunderous applause.

As it takes two to tango, so does it take two people to make up the most sensational tomahawk throwing act in show business. Spectators agree that the lovely young lady, standing bravely and unflinchingly as the lethal, whirling weapons smash into the boards so very close to her pretty pin-up figure, is entitled to as much credit for the performance as the great professional himself.

And that great professional, of course, is Skeeter Vaughan, mentioned previously as being not only one of the best and foremost knife throwers in the history of the art, but also acknowledged by his peers as the finest professional tomahawk thrower of his generation.

Professional tomahawk throwing, however, is only the tip of the iceberg so far as the ancient sport of tomahawk throwing is concerned. A vast army of "hatchet hurlers" in the United States and Canada alone now indulge in what has again become a widespread recreational activity. But before we discuss modern tomahawk throwing, let's look at how it has evolved.

The History of Tomahawks

Noted writers on the subject of edged weapons such as Frederick Wilkinson and the late Harold L. Peterson have pointed out that the early Franks of Gaul (now France) who fought with skill and bravery against the conquering legions of Rome some 2,000 years ago, threw a small axe called a *francisca* with considerable lethal effect. This weapon had a head about six inches long which was mounted on a short wooden shaft or handle. It must have been beautifully balanced for throwing. This device was in use well into the 12th century; one could even

36. Design of this French-patterned tomahawk can be traced 2,000 years back to the ancient francisca.

call it a forerunner of the Indian tomahawk, since some of the throwing axes traded to Indians by the early French voyagers had a basic shape quite similar to the ancient *francisca*.

The word "tomahawk" is derived from *tomahak* or *tamahaken,* which came from the language of the Algonquian Indians of Virginia during the era of Captain John Smith. It was absorbed into the English language during the early part of the 17th century, shortly after the first settlements were established on the eastern shores of what was then a part of Virginia. Captain John Smith himself is credited with recording the word in a dictionary of Indian words on which he is said to have worked.

The first contacts with iron and steel axes encountered by the Indians were during the time of the early Viking explorations. These intrepid warriors from Europe reached the shores of North America during the so-called "Middle Ages." Because these first contacts were few, however, no lasting impression was left, and it was not until about 500 years later, when the French fur traders began to filter into the northern reaches of the continent, that Indians began to obtain a few axes in return for their furs.

In 1668, the Hudson's Bay Company began extensive operations in the North American wilderness, and axes were vital trade items in their dealings with the Indians. In Florida and the Southwest, the Spanish also used hatchets and axes as trade goods during the same period of history, but the Spanish emphasis was on Catholic missions and agriculture, not trade for furs.

The greatest concentration of axe distribution during the 17th century was in the Northeast and throughout what was eventually to become New England and the Middle Atlantic States, plus the Midwest areas of Michigan, Illinois, and the Ohio territory. French, Dutch, and English traders provided most of the tomahawks then being distributed to the Indians.

In the early days of exploration and settlement, hatchets were primarily used by the Indians as functional tools and weapons. The ceremonial aspects of the weapon came much later when the pipe tomahawk was introduced. This pipe tomahawk became immensely popular almost immediately, because in addition to its utility as a weapon, it also offered the solace of tobacco. The pipe tomahawk arrived on the scene at about the time when many of the eastern tribes had been pacified to some extent by the traders and settlers.

Almost parallel in time with the pipe tomahawk, there appeared the dreaded spiked 'hawk which features a wicked spike on the back end of the weapon, making each end quite lethal. Furthermore, some 'hawks were produced for trade that offered a screw-type spike which could be exchanged for the pipe bowl used during more peaceful moments.

Originally, the axes brought from Europe and traded to the Indians were heavy things with the heads weighing two or three pounds. But as time went on, the evolution of the axe transformed it into a lighter and smaller weapon—one that was more suitable for use by hunting and war parties. It was partly due to this reason that the Indian gradually found the tomahawk more to his liking. Thus, while in warfare that occurred in the 1600s and 1700s, the Indian had used his bow and arrows along with his knife, later battles would witness more action with the efficient and deadly tomahawk.

After some grim and bloody lessons in Indian warfare, the traders, settlers, and frontiersmen also quickly adopted the tomahawk for their own protection—especially for last ditch, close-quarter combat.

For centuries, one favorite use of the tomahawk has been for sport. Frontiersmen enjoyed such sporting contests, and many a wager was made on individual skills to add spice to a throwing contest. Indians too held contests, though it may well be that 'hawk hurling contests that were staged by the Indians were mostly to sharpen their skills for when they went on the warpath.

In the same respect, state militia soldiers serving during the Revolutionary War often carried a tomahawk instead of a sword. The Continental Congress of the United States, in a resolution dated July 18, 1775, decreed that militiamen must provide themselves with a cutting sword or tomahawk, in addition to their muskets, bayonets, and all the rest of their gear for battle. In accordance with this, in the late 1700s, U.S. military repositories in western Pennsylvania and elsewhere carried tomahawk inventories numbering in the thousands.

It appears that the last time the tomahawk was used in Indian conflicts was at the battle of the Little Big Horn, on June 25, 1876, when the flamboyant General Custer met his fate. Surprisingly, there were few reports—actually none at the time—that the victorious Sioux warriors had wielded tomahawks against their blue-clad foes. Later, one incident concerning the battle came to light, revealing on at least one occasion during the conflict that the hatchet had been used. It concerned an Indian chief named Gall, whose two wives and three children had been killed earlier in the fighting during a charge led by Major Marcus A. Reno and his men, who were part of Custer's command.

"It made my heart bad," Gall explained when recounting his part in the battle against Custer. "After that, I killed my enemies with the hatchet!"

This apparently is the last time the tomahawk was used in Indian battles, for while the widespread use of this great weapon had been undiminished for centuries, it declined around the mid-1800s when more efficient, fast-firing guns were developed. Thus, the tomahawk as a weapon gradually faded into disuse—although during the late 1800s, the tomahawk was, of course, still used by the Indians for ceremonial purposes, or when the peace pipe was smoked at treaty ceremonies. But as a fighting weapon, the instrument fell into disuse for about 100 years or more.

The next recorded use was during the Vietnam conflict, when the LaGana 'hawk saw action. The "Vietnam tomahawk" was so named by its inventor and promoter, Peter S. LaGana. It was a lightweight 'hawk, hand-forged and with a fairly short handle. Pete LaGana sold it by direct mail to American servicemen stationed in Vietnam—or headed there—through his now defunct American Tomahawk Company. This weapon was intended primarily for self

37. The "Vietnam tomahawk."

protection in close-quarter combat situations. Apparently, as the war went on, stories filtered back to LaGana that on several occasions, it had proven itself in battle. Considerable publicity was given to this little tomahawk at the time because it had been at least a century since the weapon had been used to deliver death to a foe.

As we mentioned earlier, tomahawks can be regarded as a truly American development. There are a number of varieties according to style or design, with some made of iron, steel, or brass, and sometimes a combination of all three metals.

In museums around America, there are splendid collections of tomahawks dating back hundreds of years. The variety of design is quite amazing. Some of the decorated heads and handles are beautifully embellished with inlaid gold, silver, turquoise, brass, and sometimes fine gems. On many, there will be a heart design pierced through the blade; some feature a heart with a twisted point at the bottom that interestingly enough is said to symbolize the fifth wound of Christ.

The history of the tomahawk has indeed been rich. It has been around for more than 300 years, and in addition to its utilitarian value as a chopping tool, it has been widely used in times past with grim efficiency in hand-to-hand combat and for close-quarter personal protection. Even today, two phrases in the English language remain as reminders as to how important the hatchet has been in history. They are: "taking up the hatchet," which originally referred to when the Indians went on the warpath, and "burying the hatchet," which refers to when they made peace.

Tomahawks of Today

Tomahawk Types. Most of the tomahawk throwing done today in competition is included in the activities of black-powder muzzleloading shooters, the primary devotees to the sport of tomahawk throwing. Both knife and tomahawk throwing matches for prizes and awards are staged by these muzzleloading groups at their big invitational "shoots," which are held often in various parts of North America.

Interest has grown steadily since the early 1960s, when many such contests were started, especially

38. *Left to right:* squaw-axe with rounded poll; spike tomahawk; hammer poll; and pipe tomahawk.

among groups in Michigan and Indiana. Since those
days, tomahawk throwing competitions have in-
creased by tremendous strides as more and more
individuals participate—evidence that there is a
greater awareness of the enormous potential for
sport and recreation available to them, both within
the black-powder organizations, and as a backyard
activity. Many sources for good, inexpensive throw-
ing-tomahawks can be found, mostly available
through muzzleloading supply houses and mail-
order firms.

There are four main types of tomahawks used most
often today in muzzleloading and other forms of
competition. These are the spike tomahawk, the

pipe tomahawk, the hammer poll, and the "squaw-axe." This last model has a rounded poll—minus pipe or spike or hammer. It is a more simple and easier type to produce than the others mentioned and likewise is usually less expensive to purchase or have made.

"Squaw-axes" were so named because they were basic, lightweight hatchet types, simple in design, and used mostly by Indian squaws in the old days for mundane household chores like cutting firewood.

There was also one other type of 'hawk called a spontoon. It was a rather delicate war hatchet with a lancehead point but without a cutting edge like the other types. It was mostly a ceremonial weapon and never achieved any real popularity or widespread use. Nowhere near as good or practical as the other tomahawks, the spontoon is never seen as a throwing 'hawk in muzzleloading contests of the present day.

Those attending or participating in any of today's major invitational shoots will find sizable and enthusiastic groups of muzzleloaders actively engaged in throwing competition—both with knives and tomahawks. A careful observer, however, will seldom see two tomahawks exactly alike, since many shooters make their own, or obtain one by some judicious swapping or cash outlaying. And even though every shooter owns a tomahawk, it is surprising to see how few throwers there are who really know what constitutes a truly efficient 'hawk design—one which if properly designed and strongly made could improve their skills.

For throwing competition it is important that a tomahawk have certain design features which can provide superior performance when thrown by a 'hawk hurler of even average skill. The weight of the 'hawk head is one important feature, and for proper control of the weapon, handle length is also extremely important. Anywhere from 1 pound up to 1½ pounds for the overall weight of the tomahawk seems average for most models, and those which weigh from 20 to 24 ounces seem to outperform the lighter models.

Obviously, there are only two complete parts to this effective but primitive weapon—the head, and the shaft or handle. The blade may have either a straight or curved cutting edge with the corner nearest the hand called the "heel" and the upper corner of the blade the "leading edge." For competition, it is that leading edge which, if properly thrown, sticks into the target wood. For a simple overhand one-turn throw, the handle should extend downward at approximately a 45-degree angle from the vertical face of the target.

Many throwers use 'hawks in competition with long handles that are up to 20 inches overall. Better control of the weapon can be obtained by cutting the handles down to a more manageable length of 15 or 16 inches. Another benefit of shortening the handle is that it brings the thrower closer to the target for the single spin. This is a tried and true fact and a bit of experimentation by the thrower will undoubtedly prove well worth the time.

A properly designed tomahawk can give a thrower a big advantage in competitive throwing if he has the leading edge—that upper corner—swept up so that it extends about one inch above the top line of the head. This provides a greater sticking radius on the 'hawk and will enable the weapon to penetrate and hang in the wood even if the handle extends outward at a right angle to the vertical face of the target.

Another feature important to good design is to have the eye of the tomahawk, through which the handle is inserted, deep enough to prevent frequent handle breakage—a curse to most 'hawk hurlers! A deep eye of from $1\frac{1}{2}$ to 2 inches from top to bottom will save many a handle from breaking just below the eye. Good design should be incorporated into the shape of the eye itself to keep the handle secure and tight. Some 'hawk makers who specialize in primitive throwing models, such as the Amish blacksmiths of the Ohio River valley, forge in at least a one degree drift downward, so that when the tapered handle is inserted from the top it will have a tendency to tighten itself when the 'hawk is used.

During the 1700s, many of the larger Indian encampments boasted a resident white blacksmith who not only repaired broken gunlocks and tools, but also forged out crude hatchets and tomahawks.

The method used by these frontier craftsmen was first to hammer-fold a sheet of red hot steel or iron around a steel rod—usually an old rifle barrel—to make the eye. The two sides were then hammered and welded together, after which came the shaping, by forging, until the desired design of the 'hawk was obtained. Final steps were to grind a sharp edge and then fit a handle to the head.

This same method is used today by the Amish blacksmiths, who because of their religious convictions, do not use electric power or modern machinery to handcraft their tomahawks. They use modern cold-rolled steel to be sure, but they also insert an "edge" of tempered plowshare steel between the two layers of hot steel, and then hammer and weld the weapon to the proper specifications. The bulk of their product is made primarily for the muzzle-loading trade.

Many good modern tomahawks are made by either investment casting, or by the "lost wax" casting process which makes fine detailing possible. Then the edge is tempered to prevent cracking or chipping. Many smaller producers still forge the blades, and then make the eye from steel pipe to which the blade is welded, along with, in some cases, a spike or pipe bowl on the back of the head.

Targets. Before a 'hawk hurler can start to throw, it is necessary to obtain a proper target. Since there is nothing in the line of throwing instruments such as knives, ice picks, spikes, or screwdrivers that will tear up a target as quickly as a tomahawk or even an ordinary hatchet, it is recommended that the thrower use a large cross-section of a log for a target. With this target, throws are made into the end grain. This makes the best of all possible tomahawk backstops—especially willow—since the cross-section can be resurfaced when necessary by a sizable crosscut saw or chain saw. Power-company crews often cut down large trees with trunks wide enough to make excellent tomahawk backstops when sliced into slabs eight or ten inches thick. Bull's-eyes can either be painted on or cut out of paper. Old playing cards and paper plates make good targets too. With a bit of practice the thrower will soon be able to cut those marks to pieces. Practice, however, is the key word!

Throwing. The easiest and best way to learn how to throw a tomahawk is to stand about four long paces away from the target. A right-handed thrower should take a stance with his left foot forward and grip the handle of the hawk firmly—the same way he would grip it if he intended to split firewood. He then extends the arm holding the 'hawk and sights the bull's-eye by lining it up along the inside of the blade. Next, he swings the weapon up, back, and then forward, releasing it at the exact moment he instinctively knows that it is lined up with the mark. The throw does not need to be hard and fast as with a

39. The author demonstrating the backward, single-spin tomahawk throw.

throwing-knife, because the weight and balance of the 'hawk will do most of the work once it is properly in motion from the release. Left-handed throwers can simply reverse the stance and method just described.

It does take practice to determine accurately the correct distance to stand away from the target for a perfect stick. In the same way as determining the range for sticking a throwing-knife, you may have to move forward or backward a bit until you find the best spot on which to stand for the throw. If the distance and throw are both correct, the 'hawk's leading edge should penetrate the wood firmly. The handle should then be extending downward from the vertical face of the target at an angle of approximately 45 degrees.

When these basics are mastered—with or without coaching—the 'hawk hurler will soon be able to move back a few paces and practice throwing doubles or even the underhand single flip.

As with knife throwing, it is necesary and extremely important to follow the rules of safety. Tomahawks, like knives, can sometimes take a bad bounce and possibly injure a spectator who crowds in too close to the throwing area. Children, especially, need supervision when a knife or tomahawk competition is in progress. Always play it safe.

Besides competition, tomahawks are also used by hunters, and, of course, by performers. There are many records of even game hunters enjoying success with tomahawks. Peter S. LaGana has taken many a woodchuck in the Pennsylvania woods by hurling his lightweight hunting-fighting 'hawk with a sidearm throw. His style of sidearm throwing is similar to that of natives in the African Congo, who bring down game in much the same way with a thin, flat, multiple-pointed and many-edged throwing weapon called the "hunga-munga."

As a youth on a Cherokee reservation, Skeeter Vaughan also put meat on the table by downing several varieties of game with his knives and tomahawks. And then there is Tony Cascarella, a fearless hunter whose story will be told in detail in the next chapter, who has also killed dangerous game with his tomahawks in the swamps near Lake Wales, Florida.

Quite a number of outstanding professional throwers also perform with tomahawks as part of their acts, including Paul LaCross, Sylvester Braun, Larry Cisewski, Fritz Brumbach, and, of course, Skeeter Vaughan. One stunt especially worthy of mention was performed by the late Frank Dean who had a spectacular act involving fire hatchets. He would use a common hardware-store hatchet and shorten the handles to about 12 to 14 inches in overall length. To the back end, he would wire on a short wick, like those used in kerosene lamps, and then he would saturate the wicks with paint thinner or other flammable liquids. When ignited and thrown around his assistant, the hatchets would blaze with a yellow, slightly smoky flame. Of course, Dean would make sure that it did not burn so fiercely as to endanger that pretty girl outlined by the weapons.

For novelty, the sportman thrower can do the same stunt using pipe tomahawks, to which wicks can be easily attached. I would, however, advise you to stage the performance without the help of someone standing against the target boards: the dangerous stuff should be left to the pros.

The tomahawk is a most pleasurable weapon for amusement and recreation out in one's backyard. Many 'hawk throwers, who are not muzzleloading enthusiasts, enjoy the sport in that very manner. It is recommended that any sportsman who has never attempted the twin sports of knife and tomahawk throwing go out and try them. Both are fun, inexpensive by comparison to most other sports, and a recreational activity hard to beat!

VII
The Hunt for
the "Hog Heaven" Boar

THE VICIOUS wild boar looked as big as a lion as it charged out of the Florida swamp and headed straight for Tony Cascarella. Its six-inch curved tusks, sharp as knife blades, were already well bloodied from killing two dogs and slashing a third back in the wet brush.

Tony whipped his arm back and hurled his one-pound Tru-Bal Bowie-Axe throwing knife with full force at the 275-pound monster charging at him. The razor-sharp knife made one full turn in flight, struck the beast squarely between the eyes, and penetrated the skull. The boar stopped in its tracks and began turning around in a tight circle in a sort of death dance.

"Big T," as Tony is often called, snapped out a second Bowie-Axe, threw, and stuck the big pig in the side of the neck. He drew a third from his shoulder rig and threw again—this time sticking the boar on the opposite side of its neck as it turned, so that it appeared as though the critter was spouting a pair of metal horns, or wings, just at the back of its head.

At this point the boar dropped dead. The first throw would surely have killed it in less than a minute, but with amazing skill and accuracy, Tony Cascarella made doubly certain with the two additional perfect throws.

This was the largest wild pig ever taken by a throwing-knife hunter, and only the third known such "kill" on record. The first wild boar was also killed with a Bowie-Axe throwing knife by the late Dr. Theodore David in March of 1968. His was a small specimen that weighed just about 50 pounds, but it was the first such kill reported.

Using a matching set of four Bowie-Axe knives, Tony Cascarella went knife hunting for boar on December 28, 1975 and killed his first quarry with the knives on that date—180 pounds of four-legged fury. His second kill, to be described in greater detail, was made on March 6, 1976, and was the 275-pound monster. Later that same day, Tony went out again, armed with a pair of tomahawks, and killed another boar with two perfect throws from about 15 feet. He placed both 'hawks side by side into the pig's right shoulder, killing the 150-pounder on the spot. This was the first recorded kill of a wild boar with a thrown Indian tomahawk.

40. Tony Cascarella and his harness for holding his Bowie-Axe knives.

With two "firsts" in just one day, Tony was happy as a lark. He had also proved once again the lethal effectiveness of both throwing-knives and tomahawks in bringing down big, dangerous game when the weapons are hurled by skilled and experienced hunters.

All of these kills were made in the swamps of Florida, although the exact location of Dr. David's kill in 1968 is not known. Tony Cascarella accomplished his successful hunts with knives and tomahawks on a 5,000-acre private game preserve known as "Hog Heaven" located on Brahma Island in the middle of Lake Kissimmee, Florida, about 25 miles east of the town of Lake Wales.

"Big T" is also an expert with many types of ancient weapons, and besides his phenomenal skill with a knife and tomahawk, he is also an accomplished archer, muzzleloader, and crossbow shooter, as well as a talented master of blowguns, slingshots, and spears. A veteran of the Korean War, he first learned the art of knife throwing as a rookie soldier stationed at Fort Dix, New Jersey. He recalls that his instructor there was none other than the legendary John Styers, whose great book, *Cold Steel,* is a classic on the art of close-quarter combat.

As a boy in his home state of New Jersey, Tony received his first archery lessons from none other than Howard Hill, the king of big game bowhunters of that period. Shooting his bow with professional accuracy, Tony has killed at least 15 sharks—not to mention the many deer, snakes, foxes, wild turkeys, wild boar, leopard rays, channel bass, tarpon, and other fish, fowl, and game that have fallen prey to his amazing skill as a bow hunter.

But the throwing-knife! This is where "Big T" absolutely excels.

On his first knife hunt for wild boar in December 1975, he went hunting with only the knives—more or less on a dare from his hunting companions. With hunting on the Brahma Island preserve limited to wild boars, many archers, muzzleloaders, and conventional rifle hunters are attracted to the place;

however, what one must remember is that no one before Tony ever attempted to hunt this dangerous game with only throwing-knives. It takes a hunter of guts and determination to go after one of these mean killers that when angered or wounded will charge like a tiger. Their long tusks—up to six inches or more in length—are sharpened by constant rooting among oak roots and palmeto scrub. They can slice up a hunter, often fatally, in mere seconds.

In Florida, hunting dogs used for boar hunting are usually pit bulls or a special breed called a "Florida cur dog," a combination of redbone hound and pit bull. But even these quick and very tough dogs are easy prey for a charging boar and often are killed.

On his first hunt, Tony threw his Bowie-Axe knife at a distance of approximately 75 feet (later paced off and recorded), and had a perfect hit when the big knife sliced into the boar behind its right shoulder.

This represented a multiple spin of at least six complete turns, and although Tony had been practicing long and hard for weeks prior to this hunt, scoring such a perfect hit point first admittedly involved considerable luck as well as skill. While the first throw slowed the pig down quite a bit, with unbelievable stamina, this very strong animal immediately charged. Tony barely had time to jump back into the hunting jeep with his friends before the boar slammed its tusks into the rear wheel.

The jeep took off in a wide circle to get between the pig and the swamp. Tony jumped to the ground again and at a distance of slightly less than 50 feet hurled another Bowie-Axe and nailed the critter squarely under the neck, penetrating the chest cavity and killing it instantly.

On March 6th, about nine weeks later, "Big T" was ready to try for an even larger specimen. With the three dogs circling ahead, Tony and his hunting companion, Roy Robertson, penetrated the swamp and jumped the really big one. Hearing the commotion up ahead as the first two dogs were killed and mutilated by the boar, they plowed through the wet, swampy underbrush to try and rescue the third dog—Roy's special pet—which had already been dangerously gashed across the chest.

Tony grabbed the wounded dog just as the pig started to charge them, and literally threw it to Roy. He lost his footing as he stepped back and fell backward into the waist-high swamp water, losing his eyeglasses in the process. Roy immediately picked up a fallen tree branch and hurled it at the hog, thus turning the animal away.

Not stopping to search for his lost glasses, Tony scrambled to his feet and followed his friend as they hacked their way through head-high underbrush to reach firmer ground at the edge of the swamp.

To hell with the rattlesnakes, Tony thought, since to a wild boar, any snake is as tasty as an ice cream cone, and the poisonous reptile population is—fortunately for Tony at the moment—kept to a minimum on Brahma Island.

41. Tony ready to throw at the charging boar, now being worked by the dogs.

Upon reaching more open ground, Roy yelled, "Watch it, Tony. He'll be coming out any second now!"

"I don't know about this," Tony replied. "I lost my damn glasses back there and can't see too good. Things are kind of blurry."

"What do you want me to do, Tony? Shall I shoot it?"

"No!" Tony yelled back. "I'll take a chance with the knife. If I miss him, then go ahead and shoot."

At that moment the boar tore out of the brush not more than 15 feet away—but fortunately, though, it was not running toward them.

Suddenly, it turned and charged straight at Tony, but by this time, he already had a Bowie-Axe out of

42. Tony with his 275-pound wild boar.

his hip sheath and was ready to throw. At a range of about 20 feet, he threw the heavy knife, trying for a neck stick.

There was a clang like metal on metal, or perhaps metal on wood. For a moment, Tony thought he had missed the charging boar and hit a log or rock with the knife. But it was a perfect throw, point first, right between the eyes! With a gaping wound in its forehead where the weapon had penetrated, the big hog stopped, staggered, and began its circling dance of death. Tony rapidly followed with two over-the-shoulder knife draws and these successful sticks in each side of the big boar's neck caused its quick demise.

After hauling it back to camp, they discovered that it weighed an amazing 275 pounds. What's more, it was not even necessary to bleed out the carcass, so well had the big Bowie-Axe knives done the job. Although not the largest wild boar ever killed at "Hog Heaven," it was the largest—anywhere—ever taken with a thrown knife!

The kill itself was witnessed by the renowned big game hunter, Dr. Messer, who had just returned from an African safari hunt. He solemnly shook Tony's hand and said, "I've hunted big game for 15 years all over the world, but I have never seen anything to top this. Thanks for the show!"

So you, as a potential game hunter with the thrown knife or tomahawk, can see that with the tempered steel courage of a knife thrower like "Big T," it is possible to go after big, dangerous game. But on the other hand, it can readily be stated that a hunt like the one just described is not for everybody!

VIII

The Other
Throwing Instruments

THROWING KNIVES and tomahawks are no doubt of special interest to readers of this book, but there are many other weapons made for throwing which are still in use around the world. It should be remembered that these are of tremendous importance to many people who still use them for hunting or combat.

The list of such weapons is rather lengthy, but the ones most widely used today are the various forms of the Japanese *shuriken* and *shaken,* the boomerangs of Australia, the *bolas* of the Argentine pampas, the flat throwing-knives and spears of Africa, the lasso animal-catchers of both North and South America, and the throwing sticks used by certain American Indian tribes and some primitive peoples in other parts of the world.

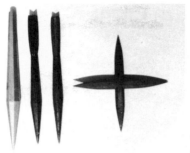

43. Three Negishi-ryu
and one juji shuriken.

The Shuriken and Shaken

It is the Japanese *shuriken,* in its many forms such as the star-shaped disc, the cross-*shuriken,* and the wheel-like throwing-stars called *shaken,* that are best known among the martial arts devotees of the present-day. Some confusion arises among the sources as to just what is the proper definition of the basic throwing wheel-like or disk-like object. Some call it the *shuriken* if it is cross-shaped, and *shaken* if it is star-shaped with six or eight points. *Sha,* of *shaken,* means wheel.

The dreaded assassins of old Japan, the ninja, were throwing experts with the *juji* (cross-*shuriken*), and also with the various star and disc-like objects which come in literally dozens of styles. The *shuriken* spike-like throwing-knives also are found in many variations as opposed to the throwing-stars.

The art of *shuriken* throwing is called *shuriken-jutsu.* (*Shuriken:* a pointed knife thrown by hand; *jutsu:*

44. The grip for throwing the long (Shiray-ryu) shuriken.

art.) *Shuriken* can vary from four to ten inches in over-all length, and come in at least 20 shapes or designs. Made from iron or steel, the *shuriken* are thrown by Japanese experts using different grips, depending on the length of the *shuriken* and the distance to be thrown to strike the target. They are basically spike-like in design, but some are quite elaborate with crosstails added to provide additional stability when thrown.

Modern knife throwers will feel a kinship to the *shuriken* spikes or knives, since with slight variations of the grip, they can be hurled much like any other type of throwing-knife.

Mr. Eizo Shirakami, the noted Japanese martial arts authority and author of that most excellent book called *The World of Throwing Knives* (printed in Japanese, however), has provided the fine photos showing the grips and throwing stance he uses him-self, as well as *shuriken* and *shaken* in various forms. He is one of the world's foremost authorities on the throwing instruments of Japan.

45. The correct stance for throwing the long shuriken.

46. Eizo Shirakami.

The Boomerang

Another throwing device which has achieved tremendous acceptance around the world as an object for sport and recreation is the Australian boomerang. Many people have the notion that boomerangs, as first used by the primitive bushmen of Australia, always return to the thrower after a long, circular flight path. This is not so, for the "returning" boomerang of today was designed for amusement. It is not—according to experts—the main type of boomerang used by the Australian aborigines.

The boomerang can rightly be called the first guided missile. While sticks and rocks are certainly the most ancient of all throwing instruments, it was the throwing stick that evolved over some 20,000 years into what is now called the boomerang. Many paintings in caves of early man show curved sticks that were used in the hunt and were presumably thrown; this leads one to believe that missilelike throwing sticks and early boomerangs were used in many parts of the ancient world. Although its exact origin has been lost in antiquity, some authorities claim that this whirling, spinning weapon was in use as early as 20,000 B.C. in ancient Egypt, India, Abyssinia, Spain, and later in North America, where the Hopi Indians of northern Arizona developed curved throwing sticks which were used to bring down jackrabbits and other small game.

Most of the "booms" used by the aborigines were for war and hunting and were not shaped to return

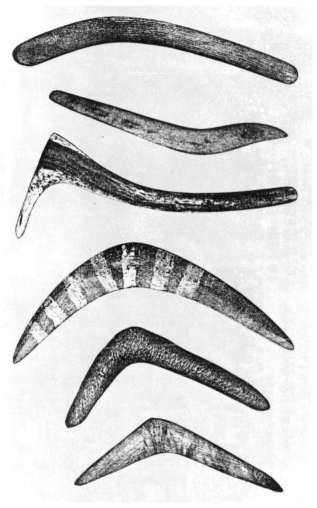

47. A museum collection of original aborigines' boomerangs.

to the thrower when the target was missed. Some had vicious outer and inner edges studded with shark's teeth or sharp stones that would maim or kill a foe on contact. The curve (angle of bend) in the long, three-foot hunting boomerangs, as well as in the even longer war weapons, was very slight as compared to the angle of bend in the returning types. The cross section was in the shape of a modern airplane wing—flat on the bottom side and with a gentle convex curve on the upper surface. When thrown, it rotated in flight as do all boomerangs, but the hunting and combat models used to bring down landbound game or foes were non-returning. On the other hand, these non-returning types could be hurled twice the distance of the returning models and some were known to have been thrown more than 200 yards.

Available more or less universally as a type of toy for sport or games, the much smaller returning boomerang is the model presently best known around the world. It would be fair to say that it does represent the most advanced form of this fascinating throwing device.

With all boomerangs, the handle arm is longer than the forward arm. A right-handed thrower should grasp the handle with the flat side toward him and the curved surface facing to his right. The opposite arm of the weapon is pointed in the direction it is to go and perpendicular to the ground. It is thrown directly forward and not upward.

The shape of the returning boomerang gives it excellent aerodynamic properties, so that as it goes forward it will turn, lift, and soar until it sweeps around in a large circle, hundreds of feet in diameter sometimes, to flutter back to the feet of the thrower. The returning boomerang must have at least an angle of 90 degrees, and is often almost U-shaped. The main use of this "boom" was to kill birds in the air and the aborigines were masters of the art, often bringing down several birds with one throw.

The Bola

On the vast grassy plains known as the pampas of South America (and especially in Argentina), the gauchos, or cowboys, of the area use a simple, but ingenious, throwing device called a *bola*. This is made of two or three stones wrapped in leather and attached to each other with leather thongs. (The two-stone *bola* is called a *somai,* and the three-stone weapon is known as *achico.*) Used to ensnare the legs of cattle, game, or running birds, the *bola* is thrown by whirling the device around the head of the thrower until sufficient velocity is built up before releasing the end of the leather thongs held in the hand.

As it flies through the air, the hide-encased stone balls separate and spread in a wide spinning circle; then when the *bola* comes in contact with the game, the balls twine around the legs of the quarry and entangle it so that it cannot escape.

The Eskimos developed a smaller type of *bola* intended to bring down birds in flight. Even some American Indian tribes used a similar device to snare birds and small animals.

The Spear

Of all throwing instruments, no doubt the spear, with all its many forms and names, was the weapon most used from the earliest times in all parts of the world. Whether it was called a spear, lance, javelin, harpoon, or African *assegai,* the same basic weapon came in many shapes and sizes. Roman soldiers threw javelins; Eskimos used harpoons for killing sea mammals and fish; African tribes had the *assegai* spear which varied in length from four to seven feet; and the ancient armies of Europe and Asia had their lances.

It was the development of the spear-thrower— also found in various shapes or designs in many parts of the world—that made the spear more deadly than most other types of throwing weapons because it added tremendous power, velocity, and distance. It was usually a short stick with a socket on one end which fitted over the back end of the spear. When snapped forward, it imparted great speed and distance to the flight of the weapon—much more than could have been generated without it.

These devices, which added so greatly to the effectiveness of the spear as a weapon, varied in design from region to region. In New Caledonia, a large Pacific island located about 750 miles east of Australia, the natives developed an *ounep*, which is a short length of cord with a loop for the index finger. On the other end is a hook or knot which is hitched around the middle of the spear and disengages at the moment of release. In New Guinea, the bamboo spear-throwers of the natives are provided with a socket. The harpoons of the Eskimos sometimes are hurled with spear-throwers which are carved with hand grips for precise control of the instrument under conditions of extreme cold and ice.

Oceania, the islands of the central and South Pacific Ocean, and the areas of Australasia, Polynesia, and the Malay archipelago, were all peopled with hunters and warriors who used spear-throwers of various types. Furthermore, spear-throwers can also be found in Africa, Mexico, and South America. What amazes researchers is the fact that even though all these throwing-weapons such as the spear-throwing devices were developed by ancient and primitive people who lived in distant parts of the world with no contact with each other, the weapons are all quite similar in design and use.

Others

Other throwing instruments of the world are not as well-known or documented as those previously described in this book, but there are a few worth mentioning. One nasty little throwing device was called the *chakram*. It came from India—home of the Gurkhas—and was a flat, steel throwing-ring with a very sharp outside edge. Although similar as a weapon to the Japanese star-shaped throwing-wheels *(shaken)*, the *chakram* was intended to cut and sever as opposed to the puncturing and penetrating action of the *shaken* and *shuriken.*

Another weapon from Australia was the *weet-weet,* or *kangaroo rat.* This was a throwing stick, pointed on both ends, that was thrown with an underhand snap or jerk. It was effective up to distances of 40 meters when hurled with speed and accuracy.

One of the most feared and deadly of the throwing artifacts to come out of Africa was the flat, thin, multi-bladed throwing-knife which has been named the hunga-munga. This weapon had points and cutting edges on all sides and was hurled sidearm, parallel to the ground, at foes or game animals. Warriors of the Congo seem to have developed this unusual throwing-knife that, like a boomerang, flies through the air with a rapidly spinning motion. This intriguing weapon can cut off the leg of a man or large game animal at distances up to 75 feet or more.

In both Asia and North America, native hunters sometimes attached tassles or streamers of leather or cloth (silk in the Orient) to the end of a knife to help stabilize the flight of the weapon. This also helped it to move more like a dart or arrow than with the usual fast spin of a thrown knife.

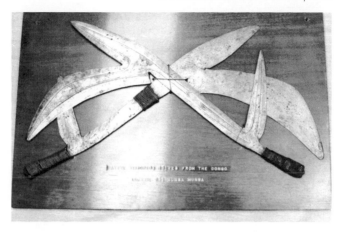

48. The "hunga-munga"—the deadly throwing-knives of Congo.

Ever since man emerged from the Stone Age, he has developed throwing weapons for hunting, war, or self-protection. Every land, in every clime, has had its share of evolution in the throwing-instruments it has used over the ages. With all due respect to the lassos of cowboys, the nets of fishermen, and others, throwing devices constructed of wood, iron, and steel—like knives, hatchets, *shuriken, shaken,* and boomerangs—are the ones that hold the most significance for all knife and tomahawk throwing enthusiasts.

IX
A Final Word

BASED ON decades of experience as a knife and tomahawk thrower and throwing-knife crafter, the author has tried in this book to provide readers with basic information regarding the art and science of throwing both types of weapons for sport, recreation, competition, and hunting.

The techniques described have proven themselves over a period that spans half a lifetime. During World War II, this writer, as an army Air Force sergeant had the pleasure of instructing other G.I.'s (quite unofficially to be sure) in the basics of knife throwing. Frank Dean and Skeeter Vaughan also instructed fellow American soldiers in the fine points of knife throwing while serving in the European theater of operations. Both had been noted professional knife throwers at the time that they entered the service.

Over all these many years, like the ripples that spread from a stone cast into a quiet pond, the sportsmen who learned from the "Sergeants Three," as we later called ourselves, have passed along to others the techniques of throwing. They, in turn, have taught the skills to even more throwing enthusiasts, so that the ripples of the art continue to spread.

Since 1949, a time when the sport started to grow, I first began to produce my Tru-Balance throwing-knives for sale rather than just for personal throwing pleasure. Replacing some of the small, lightweight imported junk advertised as "throwing-knives," many properly designed and virtually indestructible new, professional models became available as early as the 1950s, and this trend did much to improve the throwing abilities of many sportsmen.

By the mid-1960s, the black-powder shooters in America's muzzleloading organizations had begun to include the twin sports of knife and tomahawk throwing competitions as an important part of their programs staged at large invitational "shoots," as well as during their regular club activities.

Today there are many thousands of sportsmen—including a number of ladies participating in the sport of throwing knives—who are quite active as knife and 'hawk throwers, either as members of an organization or as enthusiasts out in the backyard.

It was a sad loss to the sport of knife throwing when Charles V. Gruzanski died in January 1972.

49. The late Charles V. Gruzanski in action, illustrating the proper stance and follow-through for expert knive throwing.

For a dozen years before his untimely passing at the age of 38 due to a sudden illness, Chuck Gruzanski was considered to be one of the foremost Japanese martial arts authorities in the United States. As a sergeant in the Chicago Police Department, he was an instructor in self-defense at the Police Academy. Prior to his ten-year career as a Chicago policeman, Gruzanski had served nine years in the U.S. Army— six of which were spent in Japan where he mastered many of the martial arts. He was also extremely interested in knife throwing, and together with this writer, produced a small book in 1965 called *Knife Throwing as a Modern Sport.* That same year, Chuck started the first national organization for sportsmen knife throwers. Unfortunately, it was a little ahead of its time, and lasted only a couple of years in 1965 and 1966.

In 1971, when the time seemed right, I founded a new national organization for knife throwers named The American Knife Throwers Alliance. With the help of the late Carmen Corrado of the famous Corrado Cutlery Store in Chicago, AKTA grew to have a North American membership of more than 1,200 enthusiastic sportsmen knife throwers. A quarterly newsletter, *The Bullseye Buster,* was published for 22 issues before publication had to be suspended. With very limited help or facilities, it became too big a task to produce and mail. AKTA, however, lives on, for once a member, always a member! Among the many things it accomplished,

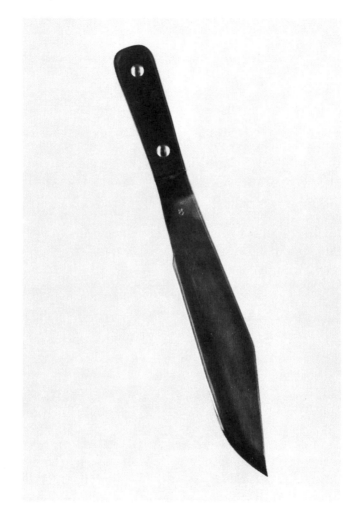

50. A 15-inch long Bowie-Axe Bolo made by Tru-Bal Knives. This design is intended for throwing by the handle grip only.

the organization achieved its primary goal, which was to provide a blueprint for organizing the sport at local levels, to offer guidelines for competition, and to serve as a clearing house for information concerning all aspects of the sport. AKTA was, and is, dedicated to promoting the art of knife throwing as a sport, recreation, and hobby.

Edged weapons of every type hold a fascination for many people, but the throwing-knife with its abundance of interesting designs and forms, along with the fabulous tomahawk, possess special qualities well-loved and respected by generations of throwers. May those folks who read this book get out and throw these two great weapons for sport and recreation, and find the same pleasure and enjoyment already discovered by previous generations.

Afterword

Many of the great professional knife throwers of the past few decades are now gone, and with them much of the raw excitement of the "impalement arts." This form of entertainment seems to have given way to more contemporary amusements, but "virtual reality" can never really compare to the frenzied energy of an up close impalement exhibition. The name itself is a misnomer, however. There is no impaling in an impalement act. As my friend the great Kenneth Pierce ("Che Che White Cloud") would say, "after all, I'm trained to miss," and "miss" he does but with heart pounding excitement in every throw. Although now in semi-retirement, Che Che is still arguably the fastest professional knife thrower performing today—and continues to be a solid advocate for recreational knife throwing as well. Knife and 'hawk throwing is truly great fun. Likewise, we hope that this book has been enjoyable reading, amusing as well as instructional. And now—if you haven't already tried it, pick up a good throwing knife or tomahawk, select a safe target and give it a hurl!

Steve McEvoy
Grand Rapids, MI
January 2004

Harry K. McEvoy founded the Tru-Balance Knife Company in Grand Rapids, Michigan in 1949. Today, Tru-Balance is one of the primary suppliers of quality throwing-knives to professionals and sportsmen alike. Harry coached and demonstrated knife and tomahawk throwing for more than 30 years and was the founder and national director of The American Knife Thrower's Alliance.

ABOUT TUTTLE
"Books to Span the East and West"

Our core mission at Tuttle Publishing is to create books which bring people together one page at a time. Tuttle was founded in 1832 in the small New England town of Rutland, Vermont (USA). Our fundamental values remain as strong today as they were then—to publish best-in-class books informing the English-speaking world about the countries and peoples of Asia. The world has become a smaller place today and Asia's economic, cultural and political influence has expanded, yet the need for meaningful dialogue and information about this diverse region has never been greater. Since 1948, Tuttle has been a leader in publishing books on the cultures, arts, cuisines, languages and literatures of Asia. Our authors and photographers have won numerous awards and Tuttle has published thousands of books on subjects ranging from martial arts to paper crafts. We welcome you to explore the wealth of information available on Asia at **www.tuttlepublishing.com**.